CAMPAIGN 298

THE FIRST AFGHAN WAR 1839–42

RICHARD MACRORY   ILLUSTRATED BY PETER DENNIS
Series editor Marcus Cowper

First published in Great Britain in 2016 by Osprey Publishing,
PO Box 883, Oxford, OX1 9PL, UK
1385 Broadway, 5th Floor, New York, NY 10018, USA
E-mail: info@ospreypublishing.com
© 2016 Osprey Publishing Ltd

OSPREY PUBLISHING IS PART OF BLOOMSBURY PUBLISHING PLC

A CIP catalogue record for this book is available from the British Library.

ISBN: 978 1 4728 1397 8
PDF e-book ISBN: 978 1 4728 1398 5
e-Pub ISBN: 978 1 4728 1399 2

Editorial by Ilios Publishing Ltd, Oxford, UK (www.iliospublishing.com)
Index by Zoe Ross
Typeset in Myriad Pro and Sabon
Maps by Bounford.com
3D bird's-eye views by The Black Spot
Battlescene illustrations by Peter Dennis
Originated by PDQ Media, Bungay, UK
Printed in China through Worldprint Ltd.

16 17 18 19 20   10 9 8 7 6 5 4 3 2 1

DEDICATION

To my father Patrick Macrory (1911–1993) who first inspired my interest in
Afghan history

ACKNOWLEDGEMENTS

I am very grateful to those who have given me support and advice. In
particular, I would like to thank the following for their generosity and
expertise: Mark Currie (School of International Relations, University of St
Andrews) Nancy Dupree, Farukh Husain (Silk Road Books), Brigadier Bill
Woodburn, Sam Astill (Somerset Museums Service), Ian Hook (Essex
Regiment Museum), Stuart Reid, and Peter Nahum (Leicester Galleries)

ARTIST'S NOTE

Readers may care to note that the original paintings from which the colour
plates in this book were prepared are available for private sale. The
Publishers retain all reproduction copyright whatsoever. All enquiries
should be addressed to:

Peter Dennis, Fieldhead, The Park, Mansfield, Notts, NG18 2AT, UK
magieh@ntlworld.com

The Publisher regret that they can enter into no correspondence upon this
matter.

THE WOODLAND TRUST

Osprey Publishing are supporting the Woodland Trust, the UK's leading
woodland conservation charity, by funding the dedication of trees.

CONTENTS

The Great Game and Afghanistan, early 19th century

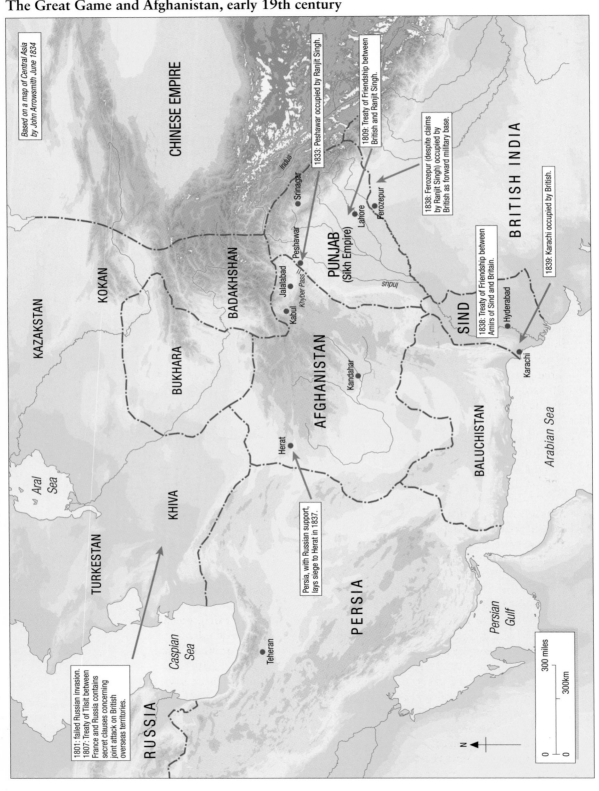

Based on a map of Central Asia by John Arrowsmith June 1834

CHINESE EMPIRE

1833: Peshawar occupied by Ranjit Singh.

1809: Treaty of Friendship between British and Ranjit Singh.

1838: Ferozepur (despite claims by Ranjit Singh) occupied by British as forward military base.

1839: Karachi occupied by British.

1838: Treaty of Friendship between Amirs of Sind and Britain.

BRITISH INDIA

Indus

Srinagar

Peshawar

Lahore
Ferozepur

PUNJAB
(Sikh Empire)

Jalalabad
Khyber Pass

Kabul

Indus

SIND

Hyderabad

KAZAKSTAN

KOKAN

BADAKHSHAN

BUKHARA

AFGHANISTAN

Kandahar

Karachi

Arabian Sea

BALUCHISTAN

Aral
Sea

KHIVA

Herat

Persia, with Russian support, lays siege to Herat in 1837.

TURKESTAN

PERSIA

Persian
Gulf

Caspian
Sea

Teheran

1801: failed Russian invasion.
1807: Treaty of Tilsit between France and Russia contains secret clauses concerning joint attack on British overseas territories.

RUSSIA

300 miles

300km

N

0

0

OVERVIEW

The First Afghan War was a political failure costing thousands of lives – British, Indian and Afghan. The British Government wished to protect the north-west borders of occupied India from perceived threats from Persia and Russia, and was intent on ensuring that Afghanistan remained an independent buffer state friendly to its interests. Poor intelligence and the need to keep other allies in the region on side persuaded the government that a regime change was needed – the existing ruler Dost Mohammad would be deposed and substituted with a former king, Shah Soojah. It was wrongly assumed that Soojah would be warmly welcomed by the Afghans as a more legitimate ruler, and that the British military could then rapidly withdraw once he had been restored to power.

Three years later, the main British force in Kabul, some 4,500 troops and 16,000 camp followers, was forced by Afghan tribal leaders to negotiate a retreat back to India but, during the march, they were all but destroyed in a little over a week. The Army of Retribution was sent the next year with the sole aim of recovering Britain's loss of pride as by then Britain had decided to abandon any further interference in the government of Afghanistan. Dost Mohammad returned to his throne and, despite what had happened, remained largely friendly to British interests until his death 20 years later.

Whatever the weaknesses of the initial political decisions taken, the undertaking in Afghanistan provides many salutary lessons concerning the conduct of a military campaign, some of which have an uncomfortable contemporary resonance. The invasion of Afghanistan by the Army of the Indus almost came to grief through poor logistical planning. There were immense difficulties in maintaining long lines of communication, and it could be said that the expedition reached Kabul more through luck and the lack of organized Afghan resistance than through the use of a carefully executed strategy. Within the East India Company there had been the fairly recent development of a political cadre, and their precise role, and the demarcation of authority between the political offciers and the military, was often unclear, leading to considerable tensions. The subtle nature of Afghan tribal leadership, where authority was based largely on consensus, was difficult for those more familiar with conventional hierarchical institutions to understand, and the British tactics of playing one tribe off against another with offers of bribes was not sustainable in the long term.

Once in occupation, the decision to place small defensive penny-packet garrisons around the country, often in hostile territory with poor communications, was one of considerable risk. The siting and construction of the British cantonments in Kabul appeared to give little thought to any defensive needs, and the British position was not helped by a continual squeeze on financial support from London. In a military crisis, effective leadership is everything, and General Elphinstone, in command of British forces at the time of the initial insurrection in Kabul, was clearly the wrong person to handle the situation. Whatever his personal qualities of humaneness, he was simply unable to make the decisive military response needed. Once the withdrawal of the British forces had been negotiated, the logistical implications of handling the enormous number of camp followers accompanying the force during its retreat was never properly addressed, and proved fatal to any sense of order or effective defence against harassment and attacks.

The British military could still win in set-piece battles but, when Afghan forces used guerrilla tactics, the British were highly vulnerable. Conventional responses such as forming defensive squares were largely futile in such situations. However, it would be wrong to conclude that the British could never employ an effective military response to this type of warfare. General Pollock, in command of the 1842 Army of Retribution, demonstrated this with his focus on meticulous logistical planning, and his effective tactic of crowning heights in hostile mountainous territory to attack the Afghans from the rear and above. From a military perspective, the loss of a single brigade during the retreat from Kabul might be considered a serious but sustainable loss – 24,000 French were killed at Waterloo and 19,000 British on the first day of the battle of the Somme. However, this was the first time that such a large professional British force had been humiliated by an apparently unsophisticated and largely uncoordinated enemy. As such, the event assumed tremendous symbolic significance, and the 'destruction of the British army' as it became known revealed potential weaknesses in British colonial structures that had hitherto been unapparent.

THE STRATEGIC CONTEXT

TRIBALISM AND CIVIL WAR IN AFGHANISTAN

By the time the British began to have serious contact with Afghanistan in the early 19th century the country had experienced over 30 years of what was effectively civil war between rival factions. This internal conflict involved an extraordinarily complex array of shifting alliances and power bases, often within the same core families. However, only 50 years earlier the Afghan empire under Ahmad Shah Sadozai had been one of the largest states in the Middle East, and at the height of his power in the mid-18th century he controlled parts of present day Iran, Kashmir, the Punjab, Sind and Baluchistan. However, it is questionable whether Afghanistan could ever have been described as a centralized state under a unifying monarch, certainly in the European sense.

Tribalism was – and remains – a distinctive feature of the country. The majority of those living in Afghanistan were Pashtuns, who themselves were members of differing tribes, but other important groups existed including Hazaras, Uzbeks, Tajiks and Nuristanis. Mountstewart Elphinstone, who had made the first visit to Afghanistan on behalf of the East India Company in 1808, provided a mass of detailed information in some nine volumes about the nature of Afghan society and politics, which later formed a bedrock of information for those deciding the direction of British policy in the region. He likened the tribes to Scottish clans, but the analogy, though superficially attractive, was misleading. Notions of clan leaders based on lineage and land ownership did not reflect the far less hierarchical nature of Afghan tribes where tribal chiefs largely maintained their position by their ability to secure and distribute wealth rather than by simple birthright.

Ahmad Shah came from the Sadozai family, who were part of the important Pashtun Durrani tribe. They had gained support from other tribal groupings by mounting aggressive foreign campaigns, and had secured a personal bodyguard of Qizilbash, who had originated in Iran. The Qizilbash were never fully integrated with Afghan society, living largely in a distinct enclave within Kabul, and later becoming key administrators under subsequent rulers.

By the time Ahmad's grandson, Shah Zaman, succeeded to the throne in 1793 the stability in Afghanistan was in decline, exacerbated by the traditional practice of polygamy leading to the dominant families having large numbers of brothers and half-brothers – some 21 in the case of Shah

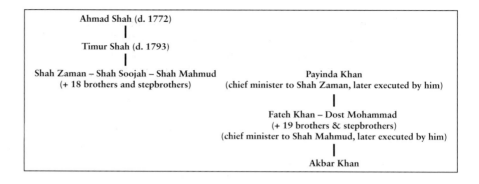

Ahmad Shah (d. 1772)
|
Timur Shah (d. 1793)
|
Shah Zaman – Shah Soojah – Shah Mahmud
(+ 18 brothers and stepbrothers)

Payinda Khan
(chief minister to Shah Zaman, later executed by him)
|
Fateh Khan – Dost Mohammad
(+ 19 brothers & stepbrothers)
(chief minister to Shah Mahmud, later executed by him)
|
Akbar Khan

Zaman – all vying for power and influence. Key rivals to Shah Zaman in the years that followed were his brother Shah Soojah, whom the British were later to support as the legitimate ruler of Afghanistan in the 1839 campaign, and his half-brother Shah Mahmud.

Shah Zaman's power base was assisted by the appointment of Payinda Khan as his chief minister. Payinda came from another important Durrani family, the Barakzais, but he tended to resist Zaman's preference for greater centralization in favour of maintaining tribal independence and loyalty. Six years after he ascended the throne, jealous of Payinda's increasing power base, Zaman had him executed. This began an extended power struggle between the Sadozais and Barakzais that dominated and shaped Afghan politics for the next 30 years. Shah Zaman's half-brother, Shah Mahmud, took control of Kabul in 1800, but three years later was ousted by another half-brother, Shah Soojah, only to return again in 1809 to recover the city. Fatteh Khan, Payinda's son, had played a key role in supporting Mahmud's recovery of his throne and was appointed his chief minister. However, history repeated itself when Mahmud had Fatteh executed in 1818 which led to an irrevocable split between the two families. In almost a mirror image of the Sadozais, Fatteh himself had 20 brothers and half-brothers, including his favourite younger brother Dost Mohammad. Fatteh's death was followed by a period of convoluted power struggles and shifting alliances, but eventually Shah Mahmud lost control of Kabul in 1818 and retreated to Herat. The following decade saw the rise of the Barakzai brothers who were equally dominated by intense fraternal rivalries and a reluctance to accept any one of them as clear leader. However, by 1819 the Barakzais had strongholds in most of Afghanistan with the exception of Herat, which continued to remain in the hands of the Sadozais.

Dost Mohammad's own power base was based in Ghazni but he gradually extended his control, finally seizing Kabul from one of his brothers in 1826. In doing this he was strengthened by marital links with the influential Qizilbash in Kabul, but even then his position was hardly secure. Significant regions of Afghanistan were never fully under his authority, notably Kohistan where Dost Mohammad had once been governor and had been particularly brutal in his rule. His elder brothers did not accept his right to rule, and essentially considered themselves as independent rulers of various territories within Afghanistan.

The decades of internal struggles had immensely weakened Afghanistan from its former powerful state, and by the early 1800s the country had contracted to include modern Afghanistan, Baluchistan, Sind, and some of the North-West Frontier provinces. External developments were an important factor in causing the country to turn in on itself. Leaders in Afghanistan had traditionally ensured loyalty by securing income for their followers. One potential source of revenue, the taxation of farming, was limited because geography restricted fertile agriculture land to areas around some of the larger cities. Instead, the traditional method of securing resources was to invade and raid external territories, especially in India. However, by the late 18th century the growing military power of the East India Company in the north of India, Persian expansionist plans from the west, and perhaps most importantly the increasing strength and ambitions of the Sikh ruler Ranjit Singh in the Punjab, effectively constrained these opportunities for instant rewards. Against this background, it is hardly surprising that during this period Afghanistan found itself increasingly dominated by internal power struggles.

RANJIT SINGH AND SIKH EXPANSIONISM

Ranjit Singh (1780–1839) was the most significant power player during the build-up to the Afghan War. Britain was maintaining the delicate balance of securing his alliance as an independent state on the northern frontiers of British India, while constraining his expansionist aims which might threaten British interests. His powerful position and subtle tactics proved critical in the final British decision to invade Afghanistan.

Ranjit Singh had become Maharaja of the Punjab in 1801, aged only 20. Over the next 25 years, he initiated a policy of unification and expansionism, initially covering the whole of the Punjab and then spreading further to include Kashmir and areas of the Khyber Pass to create a Sikh empire. Previously, untrained cavalry had formed the mainstay of Sikh forces, but Ranjit Singh's military strength lay in his development of a large professional army, modelled on European lines, and his use of European officers, often deserters or mercenaries, for training and command. His infantry and artillery were greatly strengthened, and regular troops wore uniforms along European lines. Between 1819 and 1838 the army had quadrupled in size, and by 1838 consisted of over 26,000 infantry, 4,000 cavalry, around 500 pieces of artillery, supplemented by some 10,000 irregulars, and other forces raised by levy in time of need. Ranjit Singh's reorganization of his military forces provided Dost Mohammad with the inspiration to attempt a similar move towards professionalism in the Afghan forces though on a far more modest scale.

Ranjit Singh's expansionist activities frequently brought him into conflict with Afghan leaders. Disputes over the rule of Peshawar, situated 30 miles from the southern entrance of the Khyber Pass, became a bone of contention between Afghans and Sikhs over 20 years, but in 1834, Ranjit Singh, playing on internal rivalries between Afghan leaders, formally occupied the city.

When Ranjit Singh took Peshawar, Dost Mohammad had been largely preoccupied in the west of the country where the former Afghan king, Shah Soojah, was attempting to regain his throne with a sizeable army of over 20,000 men. He had narrowly defeated Shah Soojah at Kandahar in 1833, but his military

Ranjit Singh had expanded Sikh rule alongside the north-eastern boundaries of British India, and created a formidable professional army. His long-standing antagonism with Dost Mohammad in Afghanistan meant that the British felt obliged to replace Dost Mohammad with Shah Soojah, with whom Ranjit Singh had good relations. (National Army Museum)

resources were so weakened that any immediate military campaign against Ranjit Singh at Peshawar would not have been feasible. Initially, he simply asked Ranjit Singh in the spirit of friendship to hand Peshawar back to the Afghans, but Ranjit rebuffed these overtures, and his military confidence allowed him to threaten Dost Mohammad for a share in the rule of Kabul. Dost Mohammad's reply was to force a major battle with the Sikhs at the strategically important Fort Jamrud, situated at the southern entrance of the Khyber Pass, which had been occupied by the Sikhs in 1836. In 1837 Afghan forces, commanded by Dost Mohammad's son Akbar Khan, were initially successful in reoccupying the fort, and Akbar wished to pursue the retreating Sikhs to retake Peshawar. However, faced with the Sikh reinforcements sent from Lahore, Dost Mohammad ordered the Afghan army back to Kabul. This decision was probably brought about because of the logistical problems of maintaining his force, but it was later criticized by Afghan historians as being overcautious. The battle was the last major conflict between Afghan and Sikh military forces, and Dost Mohammad subsequently relied on what was to prove unsuccessful political manoeuvring to seek the assistance of the British to regain Peshawar.

For British policy makers, the presence of a powerful Sikh state on the northern boundaries of British rule was both a blessing and a source of real concern. As an ally it could provide a valuable buffer against any threat from Russia or Persia without overextending the territorial reach of the East India Company, and a treaty of friendship had been agreed in 1809 between the British and Ranjit Singh. However, equally many policy makers considered Ranjit Singh to be a greater potential threat to British interests and the stability of the region, and there were increasing concerns about his ambitions to invade Sind, then under the control of independent Amirs with whom the British were also allied. There were also concerns as to whether, if it ever came to a conflict with the Sikhs, the British would necessarily win against such a formidable army. The Secret Committee of the East India Company noted at the time that if Ranjit Singh persisted in further expansion, 'his position would require on our part an increase in military force which would be ruinous to our embarrassed finances'.

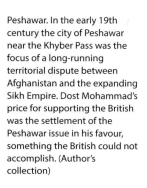

Peshawar. In the early 19th century the city of Peshawar near the Khyber Pass was the focus of a long-running territorial dispute between Afghanistan and the expanding Sikh Empire. Dost Mohammad's price for supporting the British was the settlement of the Peshawar issue in his favour, something the British could not accomplish. (Author's collection)

THE EAST INDIA COMPANY AND ITS CHANGING RELATIONSHIP WITH GOVERNMENT

The East India Company Act

The East India Company had been established by Royal Charter in 1600 as an independent privately owned company with a monopoly on trade with countries east of the Cape of Good Hope. However, by the early 19th century its relationship with the British Government had changed substantially. Company directors no longer had autonomy in how they conducted policy abroad. Pitt's East India Company Act 1784 had established a Board of Control, chaired by the Secretary of State, and stated that the Company's directors must in future 'pay due obedience to, and shall be governed and bound by, such orders and directions as they shall from time to time receive from the said Board, touching the civil or military government and revenues of the British territorial possessions in the East Indies'. Pitt was clear in Parliament as to the political shift of power involved – 'The principal object of the Act of 1784 was to take from the Company the entire management of the territorial possessions and the political government of the country.' The Company retained autonomy in its commercial activities – though it lost its trading monopoly in 1813 – but even then the Government Board of Control was entitled to access all the company's internal papers and documents. In practice, the underlying notion of the Act, that political and trading activities could somehow be divorced from each other, was hardly realistic in practice.

The East India Company Court of Proprietors. Initially established as a private trading company, the East India Company established its own powerful army to defend its commercial interests. The directors of the Company were formally responsible to the shareholders, known as the Court of Proprietors, but by the late 18th century the Government effectively controlled the Company's foreign policy and military activity. (Author's collection)

The Act went further by requiring the Company to set up a Secret Committee of up to three of its directors. The idea of a Secret Committee conducting the military affairs of the Company was not new, and the Company had set up such a committee as early as 1683. However, now the Committee would be subservient to the Government. The East India Company Act provided that where the Board of Control felt that any of its deliberations concerning war or peace required secrecy, it was entitled to send confidential instructions to the Committee. The Committee essentially formed a smaller, trustworthy conduit for the Government's interactions with the Company. At times during its existence, Committee members tried to resist or record their opposition to instructions sent by the Board, but at the end of the day the legal framework was clear - the Committee was required to comply with Government instructions.

Political and military organization of the East India Company

Following reorganizations in the early 1800s a Secret and Political Department was established as one of the five administrative divisions of the East India Company. The growing influence of the political staff within the

The Bengal Infantry. The East India Company maintained its own large military force, organized into three separate armies reflecting the three presidencies: Bengal, Bombay and Madras. By the late 18th century, native regiments outnumbered European regiments, and uniforms were increasingly fashioned along European lines. (Anne S. K. Brown Military Collection, Brown University)

Company, often recruited from the Company's army, became apparent during the build-up to the First Afghan War. Fort William College in Calcutta had been established by the Company in 1800 as an academy for oriental studies and linguistics, and in 1806 the East India Company College (located at Haileybury since 1809) was set up for the training of administrative and political staff. There were often confused lines of authority between the political and the military, leading to tensions and resentment. General Nott, using typically robust language, argued that '[t]he conduct of the one thousand and one politicals has ruined our cause', while the Duke of Wellington advised the Governor General after the British withdrawal from Kabul that the politicals had assumed far too great an influence over military strategy – 'a novelty and an abuse of modern times, arising out of jealousy of the powers of military officers'.

The East India Company had long employed its own army paid for out of its revenues, which at times was larger than the British Army. During the first half of the 18th century, the company was largely administered under three presidencies in Bombay, Bengal and Madras, each with its own army, with the Bengal President designated as commander-in-chief of the whole army. Initially, infantry regiments had been formed with European soldiers but these were increasingly supplemented by Indian regiments of sepoys commanded by European officers and NCOs, and by 1830, the total forces amounted to around 37,000 Europeans and 223,000 Indians. Organization was largely based on British Army structures, with numbered regiments of infantry, cavalry and artillery, and officers being trained at the Company's own military college in Addiscombe Place, Croydon, which was established in 1809.

As for the British Army, regiments were regularly sent on rotating tour to India, and a number of such regiments played a prominent part in the First Afghan War. There was clearly a degree of tension and snobbery between British regiments and those of the East India Company, with British Army officers rarely socializing with their counterparts in the Company forces. Senior officers from the East India Company army involved in the First Afghan War, such as General Nott, made clear their contempt for their counterparts in the British Army, especially when they thought they had unfairly been given plum commands.

RUSSIA, PERSIA AND THE BRITISH FORWARD POLICY

In the early years of the 19th century the possibility of a Russian advance from the north threatening British interests in India had begun to dominate British concerns. It was not a totally unrealistic scenario. In the 18th century, Catherine the Great, the Empress of Russia, had considered the possibility, and her son Paul, who succeeded her in 1796, had revived the idea. He approached Napoleon with plans for a joint invasion. Napoleon remained at the time unconvinced that it was militarily feasible, but in 1801 Paul had ordered an advance guard of 20,000 Cossacks to march towards India via Bokhara and Khiva. The force reached the Aral Sea, but the ill-prepared expedition narrowly avoided almost certain disaster when they were withdrawn on news of Czar Paul's assassination in Saint Petersburg.

The possibility of a Franco-Russian threat to India was revived six years later when Napoleon signed the Treaty of Tilsit with Paul's son, Alexander. The treaty contained secret clauses envisaging an alliance between France and Russia against Britain and its overseas territories. British policy makers were aware of the agreement, and a possible military threat by Russia against its possessions in India rose higher on the political agenda. Following the ill-fated 1801 Khiva expedition, there remain doubts as to whether a Russian invasion against British interests in India was ever a realistic possibility, or even seriously in the minds of Russia by the 1820s. However, continued fear of Russia's intentions caused a number of senior British policy makers to advocate a more aggressive forward policy designed to forestall any possible Russian advance by ensuring that geographically intervening states, including Afghanistan, were established as secure buffer zones.

Not all British policy makers were convinced of the need to meet Russian threats with territorial expansion. However, the position of Persia, and its willingness to shift alliances dramatically, remained a more realistic

Herat. Largely populated by Persians, the city of Herat had been seized by Ahmad Khan during the expansion of the Afghan empire in the 18th century. The Persian attack on the city, with Russian support, in 1837 strengthened the hands of British policy makers advocating a more aggressive forward policy in the region. (Author's collection)

and constant worry. Herat, on the western edge of Afghanistan, became an important focus of strategic conflict in the region. Largely Persian speaking, the city had been assimilated into Afghanistan as part of Ahmad Shah's territorial expansion. During the civil war between the Sadozais and Barakzais, the last Afghan Sadozai king, Mahmud, had taken refuge in Herat, and managed to secure its independence from both Persia and Dost Mohammad's own expanding power base centred in Kabul. The scenario suited the British who favoured the city as an independent buffer against Persian encroachment. However, the city's independence was threatened when Russia defeated Persia in 1828 following the Russian-Persian War of 1826–28. Persia remained an independent state but one that now operated under Russia's dominant influence. Persia then revived plans to retake Herat, and in 1837 sent a large army to lay siege to the city; all the evidence suggests that Russia encouraged and supported the move.

Despite its military powers, the East India Company was at heart a trading enterprise that had been drawn into political and military activities in order to protect its commercial interests. There were many senior British officials who remained unconvinced by those advocating the aggressive forward policy, and argued that expanding trade opportunities was a more effective way of protecting British interests. Lord Bentinck, who became Governor General in 1828, was a strong advocate of the so-called Indus scheme designed to open up a new route for British trade in central Asian markets in Khiva and Bokhara, providing real competition to Russian commercial trading. At the time the only effective route for British goods was by sea to Calcutta, up the Ganges river, and then overland through the Punjab towards Peshawar and the north, paying taxes and levies to local leaders on the way, and pushing up eventual prices. In contrast the Indus river could potentially provide a quicker and cheaper route for goods, and dominated British policy-thinking in the 1830s. In 1831 a 25-year-old political officer in the East India Company, Alexander Burnes, who was to later play an important role in the First Afghan War, was sent on a secret mission to survey the Indus, travelling some thousand miles and meeting with Ranjit Singh. Ranjit Singh was initially unimpressed with the prospect of the loss of revenues on existing routes, and was well aware that free commercial passage of the Indus would threaten his own expansionist plans towards the west.

Lord Auckland, who succeeded Lord Bentinck as Governor General in 1835, initially also favoured the emphasis on free trade rather than military intervention as a means of countering Russian competition. In 1836, he sent Burnes to Afghanistan to meet the then ruler in Kabul, Dost Mohammad, with clear instructions to confine his discussions to trade prospects for British goods in Afghan markets. Burnes was impressed with Dost Mohammad as a potential friend of Britain, but trying to separate trade discussions

Alexander Burnes. A political officer in the East India Company who had travelled widely in Afghanistan, Burnes failed to convince his superiors that British interests would be best met by supporting the existing Afghan ruler, Dost Mohammad. His death at the hands of a mob in Kabul in November 1841 marked the beginning of the insurrection that led to the British retreat. (National Army Museum)

from political negotiations was a near impossibility. Dost Mohammad's core obsession at the time was to recover Peshawar from the Sikhs. Various possibilities were discussed including Peshawar becoming an independent city under Dost Mohammad's half-brother, or being ceded to Afghanistan while continuing to pay tribute to Ranjit Singh. However, Burnes had no authority to offer deals on the issue, and British policy was to not unduly antagonize Ranjit Singh. As a further complication, Dost Mohammad's plans for the greater unification of Afghanistan envisaged recovering Herat, which was still under the control of the last of his Sadozai rivals, and he appeared to be planning to ally with the Persians to achieve this goal. Auckland instructed Burnes to inform Dost Mohammad that no arrangement concerning Peshawar would be acceptable to British interests. As a result the mission was a failure, though Burnes still recommended to his superiors that Dost Mohammad was Britain's best potential ally in the region.

THE BUILD-UP TO THE BRITISH INVASION

British policy was now caught up in a number of conflicting tensions and near irreconcilable goals. Despite those who advocated Dost Mohammad as someone willing to maintain Afghanistan as a friendly buffer state, it was impossible for the British to satisfy Dost Mohammad's own dispute with Ranjit Singh over the contested city of Peshawar. Worse still, Dost Mohammad was now seen to be flirting with the Russians as potentially better allies, though this was probably a bluff to improve his negotiating position with the British. Any arrangement that would unduly antagonize Ranjit Singh, with whom the British had a long-standing treaty of alliance, was not feasible, especially as he possessed an exceptionally powerful and professional army that might well be the equal to any British force. However, Ranjit Singh had his own expansionist plans towards the west that were equally as important to check. His designs on the independent Amirs of Sind were stalled when in 1838 the British concluded a treaty of friendship with the Amirs, requiring that the British mediate in any future dispute between Sind and the Sikhs. At the same time, Persia, backed by Russia, was seriously threatening the independence of Herat as a buffer to the west. A number of other conflicts in the region were also presenting challenges to overall stability. Ten years earlier threats to the north-eastern territories of British India had led to the Burmese War of 1824. Following the Anglo-Nepalese War of 1814–16, Nepal was forced to cede a large proportion of its territory to Britain, but tensions were rebuilding, with the Nepalese rulers playing on local anti-British sentiment, and the prospect of another war loomed. In 1838, conflicts with China had resulted in the launch of the First Opium War, designed to secure Britain's commitment to free trade. Even within British India, there were growing signs of local discontentment with British rule.

Relying on the opening up of trade no longer seemed to be an effective option for guaranteeing British interests. In terms of the broad strategic goal of securing strong boundaries to protect British interests, Lord Auckland, the Governor General, had been given almost a free hand in developing an appropriate strategy. The Secret Committee of the East India Company had sent him instructions on 25 June 1836 couched in the broadest terms: 'to watch more closely than has hitherto been attempted the progress of events in

Afghanistan and to counteract the progress of Russian influence... The mode of dealing with this very important question ... we confide to your discretion.'

Auckland originally identified three main options. The first was to confine any defensive line to the route of the Indus, presumably involving the Amirs of Sind who were already committed as allies to the British. This could be an attractive strategy in that it involved no large-scale commitment of British forces, but it was largely a passive approach, and would have done little to contain Persian aggression. If the Persians succeeded in taking Herat, they could be expected to move deeper into Afghan territory, towards Kandahar, creating even more instability in the region. Auckland's second option was to support the existing most powerful ruler in Afghanistan, Dost Mohammad, creating an independent buffer state friendly to British interests. This was the strategy advocated by Alexander Burnes and a number of other Afghan experts within the East India Company, and Dost Mohammad appeared to want to cement closer relations with the British. However, his price for doing so was for Britain to force Ranjit Singh of the Punjab to make territorial concessions to Afghanistan, and antagonizing such a powerful ally was simply not a risk worth taking.

Auckland's third option was a regime change in Afghanistan. Officials who had long believed in a more aggressive forward policy advised that Afghanistan urgently had to be turned into a secure buffer state friendly to the British. Key players were Claude Wade, the Company Resident in Ludhiana who had long-standing strong relations with Ranjit Singh, and Sir William Macnaughten, Auckland's political secretary. Both rejected Burnes' advocacy of Dost Mohammad as an ally of the British, and urged that the former king of Afghanistan, Shah Soojah, was an obvious candidate to ensure a country friendly to British interests. Since his failed attempts to recapture his throne, Shah Soojah had been resident in Ludhiana under British protection, but critically for British interests he had long been friendly with Ranjit Singh. Shah Soojah could be presented as the legitimate king from a long line of royal family, and one with a greater right to the throne than the Barakzai Dost Mohammad, who was known to be struggling to secure unity and stability within the country.

This third option envisioned an invasion led by Shah Soojah with support from Ranjit Singh's forces, which must have appeared both logical and attractive. Shah Soojah would be indebted to the British, and would create a powerful buffer against foreign intrusion. Ranjit Singh was already an ally of Shah Soojah, and had supported his previous unsuccessful attempts to retake his throne. The arrangements could involve Shah Soojah giving concessions to the Punjab, finally settling long-standing conflicts between Afghanistan and the Punjab over Peshawar and other territories. An invasion by Ranjit Singh into Afghanistan would be a rightful revenge for the losses sustained during the battle of Jamrud only a year earlier, and would direct Ranjit Singh's expansion northwards rather than towards Sind to the west, which the British wished to keep under their influence. There would be a financial cost in supporting Shah Soojah and Ranjit Singh but no major commitment or exposure of British troops.

Not surprisingly, Auckland committed to the third option in 1838 and secured backing from London. In the first half of the year, lengthy negotiations took place between Macnaughten and Ranjit Singh, who initially appeared enthusiastic, especially if it involved a final settlement in his favour to the

Peshawar situation. The British envisaged two invading armies – one led by Shah Soojah via Sind taking Kandahar before moving on to Kabul, and the other containing Ranjit Singh's forces moving from Peshawar up the Khyber Pass into Afghanistan – creating a pincer movement around Dost Mohammad with the British providing only financial and political support. Ranjit Singh, however, played a shrewd political game, and avoided committing his forces. Memories of the heavy costs of at Jamrud in 1837, where his leading general had been killed and both sides had taken many casualties, must have warned him that any new military aggression against Afghanistan could prove costly. Some British advisers also advised against undue reliance on Ranjit Singh since Shah Soojah's claims to legitimacy would be damaged if he were seen to be directly supported by such a long-standing enemy of Afghanistan. The commander-in-chief of British forces in India, Sir Henry Fane, did not in general approve the policy of military interference in Afghanistan, but advised Auckland that if this were to happen, half measures would be inappropriate and the British military should take the lead. The decision was taken during the summer of 1838 to commit British forces to lead the invasion.

A tripartite treaty between the Government of India, Ranjit Singh and Shah Soojah was signed on 26 June 1838. The treaty confirmed Sikh control over former Afghan territories including Kashmir and Peshawar. Ranjit Singh in turn agreed to abandon any further claims on Shikarpur in the Sind in return for annual payments to be made by the Amirs of Sind (who do not appear to have been consulted about the matter) and Shah Soojah equally relinquished any claims over the region. Shah Soojah was to pay for a force of 6,000 Sikh cavalry and infantry at Peshawar to provide assistance if required. Plunder taken from Dost Mohammad was to be divided between Shah Soojah and Ranjit Singh, while Herat was to remain effectively independent under its existing governor, Shah Soojah's nephew. The terms were hardly favourable to Shah Soojah, but the prospect of at last re-securing his throne would have blinded him to the sacrifices he had been obliged to make.

Three months later Lord Auckland issued the Simla Manifesto, the public announcement justifying the British invasion. It accused Dost Mohammad of making unprovoked attacks on Britain's long-standing ally Ranjit Singh, and stated that as long as he remained in power in Kabul 'we could never hope that the tranquillity of our neighbourhood could be secured, or that the interests of our Indian Empire would be preserved inviolate'. The attack by Persia on Herat was considered to represent an expansionist strategy by Persia that would threaten British interests in the region. The situation, therefore, warranted the British espousing the cause of Shah Soojah 'whose popularity throughout Afghanistan has been proved to his Lordship by the strong and unanimous testimony of the best authorities'. Finally, in a masterpiece of wishful thinking, it concluded: 'The Governor General confidently hopes that the Shah will be speedily replaced on the throne by his own subjects and adherents, and when once he is secured in power and the independence and integrity of Afghanistan established, the British Army will be withdrawn.'

The document, though issued in the name of Lord Auckland, was signed on his behalf by William Macnaughten and no doubt the elegant text, so full of sophistry and ambiguity, had been drafted by him. The same day it was issued, notification was made that Macnaughten had been appointed Envoy and Minister for the Government of India at the court of Shah Soojah.

CHRONOLOGY

1836	Dost Mohammad appointed Amir of Kabul.		**23 July**	British storm and capture Ghazni.

1836	Dost Mohammad appointed Amir of Kabul.
1837	Persia besieges Herat with Russian support.
1838	
26 June	Tripartite agreement between the British Government, Ranjit Singh of the Punjab, and Shah Soojah recognizes Shah Soojah as the legitimate king of Afghanistan.
1 October	Simla Manifesto issued by Governor General Auckland declares the British intent to install Shah Soojah on the throne.
21 November	Bombay Column departs Bombay.
10 December	Bengal Column leaves Ferozepur.
1839	
26 March	Bengal Column arrives in Quetta via the Bolan Pass. Sir John Keane assumes command of the combined Army of the Indus (around 20,000 fighting men).
25 April	Shah Soojah enters Kandahar without resistance. The main body of the Bombay Column meets up with the Bengal Column. Coronation of Shah Soojah.
27 June	Army of the Indus departs from Kandahar.
23 July	British storm and capture Ghazni.
7 August	Shah Soojah enters Kabul accompanied by British forces. Dost Mohammad flees to the north.
18 September	British forces in Kabul reduced with the departure of the Bombay Column back to India via the Bolan Pass.
1840	
Spring	British construct cantonments at Kabul outside the city.
September	Dost Mohammad mounts a resistance.
2 November	Dost Mohammad defeats the British cavalry at Purwandurrah.
3 November	Dost Mohammad surrenders to the British at Kabul and is sent into exile in India.
1841	
9 October	Further reduction of the British forces with a brigade under General Sale leaving for the Khyber Pass via Jalalabad.
2 November	Uprising in Kabul City. Political agent Alexander Burnes murdered.
	British detachment of 130 killed at Syadabad.

4 November	Commissariat fort near Kabul cantonments attacked and abandoned.
10 November	British capture Rika-Bashee Fort near Kabul cantonments.
	Garrison of over 700 Ghurkas at Charikar destroyed.
23 November	Dost Mohammad's son Akbar Khan arrives in Kabul to take command of the resistance.
	British lose battle on Beymaru Heights and abandon artillery.
30 November	British garrison at Ghazni besieged. Garrison wiped out six weeks later.
11 December	Reinforcements from Jalalabad and Kandahar unable to reach Kabul due to hostilities and poor weather. British and Afghan leaders reach agreement for the safe withdrawal of British troops and camp followers from Kabul.
23 December	British Envoy Macnaughten murdered while trying to renegotiate new terms with Akbar Khan.

1842

1 January	New agreement reached with Afghan leaders for safe withdrawal of British forces.
6 January	British forces consisting of 4,500 troops and 12,000 camp followers in Kabul depart, starting the retreat to Jalalabad. General Nott remains with brigade in Kandahar. Shah Soojah remains in Kabul as king.
9 January	12 officers' wives, 22 children, and some officers taken as hostage.
11 January	Heavy losses of British forces and camp followers in Jagdalak Pass.

13 January	Remainder of British troops make last stand at Gandamak. Sole European survivor, Dr Brydon, reaches Jalalabad.
4 April	Shah Soojah murdered and succeeded by one of his sons.
5 April	Army of Retribution under General Pollock forces the Khyber Pass.
8 April	Sale, under siege in Jalalabad, defeats forces led by Akbar Khan, who returns to Kabul where he assumes power.
9 August	General Nott leaves Kandahar for Kabul.
14 April	General Pollock's army arrives at Jalalabad.
20 August	General Pollock leaves Jalalabad for Kabul.
12 September	Akbar Khan defeated at Tezin by Pollock's army and escapes to northern Afghanistan.
15 September	General Pollock arrives at largely deserted Kabul, followed three days later by General Nott.
19 September	British prisoners taken as hostages during the retreat released.
9 October	Destruction of the Great Bazaar in Kabul.
12 October	British forces leave Kabul via the Khyber Pass to Peshawar.
1843	Dost Mohammad reinstated as Amir.

OPPOSING COMMANDERS

BRITISH COMMANDERS

Sir William Macnaughten, Envoy to Kabul

Sir William Hay Macnaughten, the second son of Sir Francis Macnaughten, a judge of the Supreme Court of Calcutta, was born in Calcutta in 1793. Educated at Charterhouse School, he joined the Madras Army as a cavalry cadet aged 16, initially being posted to the Governor's bodyguard. Two years later he joined the 4th Cavalry at Hyderabad, but then decided to switch from a military career and joined Fort William College, Calcutta. There he proved himself to be an outstanding linguist, becoming fluent in Persian, Sanskrit, Arabic, Hindi and other Indian languages. He then joined the legal services, eventually becoming the court registrar at the highest court of appeal in Bengal, and wrote two major treatises on Mohammadan and Hindu Law.

His political career was launched in 1831 when he was appointed secretary to the Governor General of India, Lord Bentinck, during his tour of the upper provinces, and was subsequently promoted to chief secretary of the political department. He remained in this post when Bentinck's successor, Lord Auckland, was appointed in 1836. He accompanied the Governor General on his two-year tour to the north in 1837 where he developed the strategy that ultimately led to the invasion of Afghanistan, and later persuaded Lord Auckland to appoint him as Envoy and Minister to Kabul, making him the most senior political figure during the occupation and uprising.

A born bureaucrat, with a reserved and often pompous character, who was a stickler for proper form, Macnaughten gave rise to contradictory assessments at the time. Emily Eden, Lord Auckland's sister who accompanied Macnaughten on the northern tour, commented tartly that he was 'clever and pleasant, speaks Persian rather more fluently than English; Arabic better than Persian; but, for familiar conversation, rather prefers Sanskrit'. However, young officers could be devoted to him – Colin Mackenzie, for example, was 'convinced of his worth, both as a public servant and a private gentleman'. However, he was equally criticized as a desk-based civil servant, out of his depth, obstinate, and overly self-confident. Macnaughten was reluctant to hear any criticism of the invasion, and remained convinced of its strategic value during the occupation, despite the obvious signs that all was not well. Nevertheless, in the final months he showed considerable strength of character, with Sir John Kaye in his magisterial history of the Afghan War written eight years after the event commenting, 'There was but one civilian at Caubul; and he was the truest soldier in the camp.' He was murdered by Akbar Khan in 1841, while negotiating the terms of the British departure from Kabul.

Sir John Keane, Commander of the Army of the Indus
Born in 1781, Keane joined the regular army, serving in various regiments in Egypt, Gibraltar and Malta, and aged 22 became a junior lieutenant-colonel in the 13th Foot. He served in Wellington's Peninsular campaign, becoming a major-general in 1814, and subsequently commanded a brigade during the unsuccessful attack on New Orleans during the War of 1812 between Britain and America. He later commanded troops in Jamaica, and became colonel of the 68th Light Infantry in 1831.

In 1833 he was appointed commander-in-chief in Bombay, serving under Sir Henry Fane, commander-in-chief in India. Fane organized the invasion force of the Army of the Indus, and was originally intended to command it. However, due to his ill health and a reduction in the size of the army after the Persians lifted their siege of Herat, command of the army was handed over to Sir John Keane in January 1839. Whatever his reputation for personal bravery, the appointment was not without controversy. Keane was described as a man of violent temper 'who used the language of the barrack room'. More significantly, he was considered to be a King's officer, who some considered should not have commanded a force that was largely composed of East India Company troops. Keane's apparent favouritism of King's army officers led to particular tensions with Major-General Nott of the East India Company, who was probably the better soldier, though someone with equally rough manners.

Major-General Elphinstone. Against his own misgivings Elphinstone was appointed commander of the British forces in Kabul after the successful invasion. All too aware of his own weaknesses, he proved incapable of providing decisive military leadership once the insurrection in Kabul had broken out in 1841. He was taken hostage during the retreat, and died of dysentery during his imprisonment. (National Army Museum)

Following the successful invasion, Keane was recalled with a portion of the army back to India in October 1839. Two months later he was raised to the peerage as Baron Keane of Ghuznee and Coppoquin, County Waterford with a pension of £2,000 a year. He died in Hampshire in 1844.

Major-General William Elphinstone Commander-in-Chief, Kabul from 1839
Born in 1782, the son of a director of the East India Company, William Elphinstone joined the King's army, serving in various regiments, and became lieutenant-colonel of the 33rd Foot, where he fought with distinction at the battle of Waterloo. He later joined the 16th Light Dragoons, becoming a colonel in 1825, served for a period as aide-de-camp to George IV, and was promoted to major-general in 1837.

In 1839 he was appointed to command the Benares Division of the Bengal Army for what should have been a quiet retirement appointment for a man now ill and lame with gout. However, soon after, and against his protestations that he was too old and too ill – he later commented that he was 'unfit for it, done up in body, and mind' – he was nominated by Lord Auckland to succeed Sir Willoughby Cotton as commander of the remaining occupying forces in Kabul. The appointment was a surprise, but was probably in part due to Lord Auckland's underestimation of the seriousness of the situation in Kabul, old family friendships, and the tendency to favour officers of the King's army over those of the East India Company. Indeed, Nott, who had hoped that he would receive the appointment, commented that Elphinstone was 'the most incompetent soldier that was to be found among the officers of the requisite rank'.

By all accounts Elphinstone was a nice and gentle man, and all too aware of his own weaknesses. On arriving in Kabul, he was immediately aware of the poor strategic location of the British cantonments, even offering to reinforce the perimeter at his own expense. However, he lacked the military decisiveness needed when the insurrection in the city first took place, constantly consulting with junior officers, and reluctant to see soldiers come to any harm. His position was not helped by an obstructive and openly disrespectful second-in-command, Brigadier Shelton, and difficult relationships with the political envoy, Macnaughten. Trying to rally demoralized troops, he was heard to complain to Macnaughten, 'Why Lord, sir, when I said to them, "Eyes right", they all looked the other way!' Lord Auckland eventually recognized that he was too ill to continue in command, and had ordered him home to be replaced by Major-General Nott, a far more decisive soldier. However, the order came too late as the Afghan uprising had taken place only weeks before the change of command could be effected. He was amongst a number of British officers taken prisoner by the Afghans during the early days of the retreat from Kabul, and died of dysentery during captivity.

General William Nott

Born in 1783 and brought up in Wales, aged 17 William Nott joined the East India Company army as a cadet. Aged 21 as a lieutenant in charge of a detachment of the 20th Native Infantry in an expedition against Sumatra pirates, he found himself unfairly court-marshalled for refusing to obey orders to leave his position. He defended himself successfully but the experience left him with an abiding resentment as he felt he had been unjustly treated by his superiors. Throughout his career he felt that officers of the East India Company were treated unfairly compared to their counterparts in the British Army.

Following a period in England, he returned to India in 1824 and was placed in command of a number of native infantry regiments. In September 1838, he was promoted to brigadier-general and given command of the 2nd Brigade of the 1st Division of the Army of the Indus. On arrival of the troops in Ferozepur, he was temporarily put in command of the 1st Division, while awaiting the arrival of Sir John Keane, the overall commander-in-chief. He resented Sir John's appointment: 'A Queen's officer should never command in India; whatever his talents may be, he is for a thousand reasons unfit.' His pique worsened when Keane ordered him to stay with a force in Quetta while the remainder of the army moved on to Kabul. He successfully secured Kandahar, and during 1841 effectively dealt with insurrections in the area.

Despite his reputation for outspokenness, his military capabilities were recognized when he was appointed to succeed General Elphinstone as commander of the British forces in Afghanistan. However, two weeks before he was due to take up his post, the uprising in Kabul took place. Following the agreement to withdraw all British forces negotiated between the Afghan leadership and Elphinstone, Nott refused to leave his base in Kandahar, assuming the terms had been made under coercion. With the arrival of the Army of Retribution in 1842 under General Pollock, he led his forces out of Kandahar, defeating major Afghan resistance outside Ghazni, and joined up with Pollock's army at Kabul.

On his return to India, he was appointed Envoy to the King of Oude in north-east India, but at the end of 1843 he was given leave to return to Britain due to ill health and retired to Wales after being given a pension by the East India Company. He died on 1 January 1845.

General Sir George Pollock, Commander-in-Chief, Army of Retribution

Born in Westminster in 1786, George Pollock attended the Woolwich Military Academy, and aged 18 joined the Bengal Artillery at their headquarters in Dum-Dum as a lieutenant-fireworker. His early military experiences affected his subsequent approach to strategy and organization. He took part in the 1804 Mahratta War, and saw at first hand the failure of the British to take the city of Bhurtpore, a failure caused not least by inadequate preparation before the launch of storming parties. In 1814, he volunteered to take part in the Nepalese campaign, learning much about the challenges of fighting in mountainous territory.

In 1824 he was promoted to lieutenant-colonel, and took part in the Burmese campaign, commanding the British artillery, and demonstrating what would become a preoccupation with meticulous logistical planning. After the destruction of the British forces on retreat from Kabul in 1842, Pollock was appointed by Governor General Auckland to lead the so-called Army of Retribution back into Afghanistan. Again, he showed his concern for careful planning, delaying the march for several months until he felt fully prepared, and was described as a 'cool, cautious officer'. Pollock showed considerable nerve, if not flagrant obstinacy, in refusing to obey orders from the Governor General to withdraw the Army of Retribution once it had successfully taken Jalalabad. Following several months of hard negotiations, the Governor General eventually conceded that Pollock could withdraw via Kabul, where he authorized a symbolic destruction of the Great Bazaar.

Compared to the honours immediately bestowed on Sir John Keane, Pollock's recognition was more muted though he received a GCB (Knight Grand Cross), and was congratulated in Parliament by the Prime Minister. He became Envoy at Lucknow, and was appointed Military Member of the Supreme Council of India in 1844, retiring due to ill health to England in 1846. He became a member of the East India Company's board of directors in 1854. Promoted to field marshal in 1870, he was appointed Constable of the Tower of London in 1871 and a year later, in the last year of his life, was granted a baronetcy.

General Sir George Pollock. In 1842 Governor General Ellenborough appointed Pollock to lead the Army of Retribution with the aim of restoring British honour following the disastrous retreat from Kabul. A cool, careful officer with a reputation for meticulous planning, Pollock's tactics effectively defeated Afghan military resistance. (Author's collection)

AFGHAN COMMANDERS

Shah Soojah al Mulk

Born in 1785, Shah Soojah was a member of the Sadozai family from the Durrani tribe that had ruled Afghanistan since 1747. He was governor of Herat and Peshawar between 1798 and 1801 while his elder brother Zaman Shah was king. Zaman Shah was deposed during the extended rivalry between the Sadozais and Barakzais, and Shah Soojah, still in his teens, escaped arrest and fled to the mountains in the east of Afghanistan. He secured the Kabul throne from his half-brother, Mahmud Shah, in 1803, and ruled for six years attempting to reconcile the rival clans, even marrying into the Barakzais. However, by then the country was largely in a state of anarchy, and his area of effective rule had shrunk. Shah Soojah tried securing an alliance with the East India Company, but in 1809 he was deposed by Mahmud, supported by Dost Mohammad, and escaped into exile.

He unsuccessfully attempted to reclaim his throne a number of times, and in 1833 agreed to a joint invasion with Ranjit Singh in return for handing the contested city of Peshawar to the Sikhs. However, he was defeated near Kandahar by Dost Mohammad, and returned to exile in India. Under the tripartite alliance between him, the British, and Ranjit Singh, it was agreed that he would be reinstated as the legitimate ruler of Afghanistan, and supported by British troops and in command of his own force, he was enthroned in 1839. However, he did not enjoy the popular support that the British had expected, though the complex rivalries within Afghanistan meant that there were still many royalist leaders who favoured his rule over that of the Barakzais. Despite his reputation of having a degree of haughtiness, he was politically adept, and had the British withdrawn earlier he might have been in a better position to secure his rule. He remained in Kabul when the British were finally forced to leave in January 1842, and attempted with some success to secure alliances between different factions to resist the increasing power of Akbar Khan, Dost Mohammad's son. Though urged to lead his forces against the British remaining in Jalalabad, he was reluctant to do so, and in April 1842 was assassinated by a Barakzai rival.

Shah Soojah. A former Afghan king, Shah Soojah had been defeated during the civil wars that beset the country. The British decided to reinstate him as someone who would act in British interests, wrongly judging that he would be welcomed by the Afghans as a more legitimate leader than the existing ruler in Kabul, Dost Mohammad. (Art and Architecture Collection, Miriam and Ira D. Wallach Division of Art, Prints and Photographs, The New York Public Library, Astor, Lenox and Tilden Foundations)

Dost Mohammad Khan

Born in 1793, Dost Mohammad was the 20th of the 21 sons of Payenda Khan of the Barakzai clan. His elder brother, Fatteh Khan, the head of the Barakzais, had earlier joined forces with the Sadozai Mahmud Shah to overthrow Mahmud's brother, Zaman Shah. In 1809 Mahmud succeeded to the throne, with Fatteh Khan becoming chief minister and Dost Mohammad, along with his brothers, receiving other official appointments.

Dost Mohammad was known by his brothers as 'Gorgak' or 'Little Wolf', and was a favourite of his eldest brother Fatteh Khan from an early age. Aged nine he had witnessed the murder of his father by Zaman Shah, and history repeated itself when Fattah Khan was later executed by Mahmud Shah. Following complex power struggles between the remaining Barakzai brothers and stepbrothers, Dost Mohammad became governor of Kabul, Ghazni, and Kohistan where he gradually consolidated his power, and began to modernize the structure of the army. His intention was to reunify Afghanistan as a kingdom with a stronger central government but he was unable to overcome the continuing tribal strengths and jealousies of his many brothers. In 1836 he was appointed by religious leaders as Amir of Kabul, and on his first meeting Alexander Burnes was struck by the 'intelligence, knowledge and the curiosity which he displays, as well as his accomplished manners and address'.

Following his exile in India in 1839, after the invasion of the British, he returned to Kabul to resume his rule in 1843 when the British finally departed from Afghanistan. He set about professionalizing the army and unifying the country, recovering Kandahar in 1854 and Herat in 1857. He signed a treaty of friendship with the British Government in 1855, and refused to assist his fellow Muslims during the India Mutiny. He died in 1863.

Dost Mohammad Khan. Dost Mohammad emerged as one of the strongest leaders during the early 19th-century civil wars in Afghanistan, and in 1836 he was appointed ruler in Kabul. Noted for his intelligence and lack of conceit, Dost Mohammad was unable to resist the British invasion, but after the final withdrawal, returned to power until his death in 1863. (Art and Architecture Collection, Miriam and Ira D. Wallach Division of Art, Prints and Photographs, The New York Public Library, Astor, Lenox and Tilden Foundations)

Akbar Khan

Born in 1816, Akbar Khan was the fourth son of Dost Mohammad, and was in command of the victorious Afghan forces at the battle of Jamrud against the Sikhs in 1837. Married into the Ghilzai tribe, he was appointed governor of Kohistan in 1833 and Jalalabad between 1834 and 1839. He escaped with his father from Kabul following the invasion by the British in 1839, but remained in the north of the country to assist leading the resistance. A charismatic and sophisticated figure, described by General Sale's wife during her captivity following the British retreat as 'a jovial and smooth-tongued man' but one with 'ungovernable passions, and his temper when thwarted is ferocious'.

His reappearance during the insurrection in Kabul in 1841 brought leadership and more effective strategy to what hitherto had been a largely opportunistic and uncoordinated uprising, though his ascendance was not without jealously from competing relatives and tribal leaders. He helped negotiate the agreement with the British to withdraw their forces to India under safe conduct. It does not appear that he planned the wholesale destruction of the British force during the retreat but more likely that that he was unable to control more aggressive tribesmen, though in the end he did little to prevent it.

He led the Afghan resistance to the British Army of Retribution sent in 1842, but was defeated by General Pollock's forces in a major battle at Tezin on the route between Jalalabad and Kabul. Once the British Army had retired from Afghanistan he assumed temporary control awaiting the return of his father. Dost Mohammad appointed him as governor of Jalalabad and Laghman, and he retained a position as heir apparent. However, he came increasingly into conflict with his father over what he considered to be the slow progress in unifying the country, and the lack of aggressive military action against the Sikhs in the Punjab. He died in 1845 aged 29, with rumours that he had been poisoned at the instigation of his father.

Akbar Khan was the great-great-grandfather of the last King of Afghanistan, Zahir Shah, who was deposed in 1973. Today his name is still revered in Afghanistan as a nationalist leader, with a wealthy neighbourhood in Kabul (ironically adjacent to the former site of the British cantonments) named after him, together with Afghanistan's leading hospital, the Wazir Akbar Khan Hospital.

Akbar Khan was the fourth son of Dost Mohammad, and took a key role in leading the Afghan forces against the British, and negotiating the British withdrawal from Kabul. A charismatic figure and lover of poetry, he remains a national Afghan hero. (Art and Architecture Collection, Miriam and Ira D. Wallach Division of Art, Prints and Photographs, The New York Public Library, Astor, Lenox and Tilden Foundations)

OPPOSING FORCES

BRITISH FORCES

As commander-in-chief in India, Sir Henry Fane took charge of deciding the size of the force and its deployment, and on 13 September 1838 he issued a general mobilization order. The force was mainly made up of troops from the East India Company army but included some regiments of the British Army on rotational duty. A Bengal Column under the command of Sir Henry, consisting of a brigade of artillery, a brigade of cavalry, and five brigades of infantry, was to assemble at Ferozepur, the most northern cantonment town of the East India Company (and today the headquarters of the 7th Infantry Division of the Indian Army), and march some 1,000 miles through the Bolan Pass towards Quetta and Kandahar in Afghanistan. Six thousand soldiers were to be attached to Shah Soojah and accompany the Bengal Column. Though largely composed of infantry from the East India Company, under the command of an assigned British officer, it was to be designated Shah Soojah's personal force – the Simla Manifesto had emphasised that Shah Soojah would enter the country surrounded by his own troops, and it was important for his pride and the underlying politics that he was seen to

The Army of the Indus. Consisting of three forces – the Bengal Column (9,500 soldiers), the Bombay Column (5,600 soldiers), and Shah Soojah's force (6,000 soldiers) – the army set off towards Afghanistan in great style with an enormous number of animals, baggage, and camp followers. However, the expedition almost came to grief due to poor provisioning and the harsh terrain. (National Army Museum)

have some degree of independence from the British military forces. Another force of 6,000 troops was to be attached to his son, Prince Timur, under the command of a British officer. Mainly composed of Sikh soldiers and based at Peshawar, it would enter Afghanistan via the Khyber Pass towards Jalalabad. A smaller Bombay Column consisting of a brigade of cavalry, a brigade of artillery, and a brigade of infantry would travel from Bombay by sea to Karachi, and travel overland to meet the Bengal Column at Shukapur just before entering the Bolan Pass.

The combined forces, known as the Army of the Indus, numbered around 20,000 fighting men. In addition there was an enormous number of camp followers and baggage handlers who far outnumbered the actual soldiers – in the case of the Bengal Column, some 38,000, together with 30,000 camels.

AFGHAN FORCES

The Afghans had no standing army equivalent to that of the British or to Ranjit Singh's army in the Punjab. Forces were raised in times of need from tribal chieftains in return for land grants, the remission of taxes, or the prospect of plunder from aggressive expeditions. The majority of the forces available were cavalry (*khud aspa*) with around a quarter being infantry (*eljaris*). The decentralized system had inherent weaknesses, creating uncertainties in the size of force that could be raised at any particular time, with the payment systems encouraging tribal leaders to give inflated numbers when stating the forces they would raise. The system meant that underlying loyalties were to local tribes, who often were concerned with their own internal disputes with each other rather than a centralized command structure.

The Afghans had no standing army equivalent to that of the British, and forces were largely raised in times of need from tribal chieftains in return for land grants or levies. The soldier here is armed with a *jezail* the accuracy and range of which outmatched the British standard issue musket, and proved deadly. (Picture Collection, The New York Public Library, Astor, Lenox, and Tilden Foundation)

The Sadozai kings had long engaged a small bodyguard of paid soldiers, and Dost Mohammad, impressed by the way Ranjit Singh had professionalized his army along European lines, attempted to do the same, employing three foreign advisers, including a former British officer who had been attached to Shah Soojah's force. To counteract the long-standing dominance of cavalry, Dost Mohammad deliberately created infantry regiments paid by the government and which amounted to some 1,500 men. At the same time, he created a small body of 3,000 cavalry under direct central control, with pay and horses provided by the government, something unheard of before in the country. These government soldiers, however, remained very much the minority, and tribal cavalry and infantry raised in traditional ways formed the bulk of the forces available to him.

In such an uncentralized system, there was no effective commissariat. Provisioning of military forces was a constant challenge, with local communities being obliged to provide food, and

a large proportion of time was spent in acquiring provisions. In what was largely an agricultural community, seasons also had their effect, with fighting men likely to be preoccupied during harvest times. It may be no coincidence that the main British victories during the First Afghan War (Ghazni and the march to Kabul in 1839, and the battle of Jalalabad in 1842) occurred during the summer months, while the Afghans had their greatest successes (starving out the cantonments in 1842, the retreat of the British force from Kabul, and the capture of garrison outposts) during the winter.

The main firearm used by the Afghans was the long-barrelled *jezail*, which used matchlock or flintlock mechanisms. The distinctive curved stock probably added stability when firing from a horse, and while it took some time to load, a favourite tactic was to hold several loaded *jezails*, ride up and fire, then depart or dismount and continue to fight with swords or knives.

Alternatively, they were used for long-range sniping, often using a tripod, and were considered to be accurate up to 250 metres. The preferred tactic was to avoid mass volleys but to use carefully aimed fire, conserving ammunition. The range of the standard British Brown Bess musket at the time was less than half that distance. It was effective at close quarters, but made soldiers very vulnerable to Afghans sniping from cover. Ironically, in 2010 British troops in Afghanistan had to be issued with new US long-distance Sharpshooter rifles because the standard British issue SA80A2 assault rifle could not match the range of firearms then being used by the Taliban.

ABOVE LEFT
An example of an early 19th-century flintlock pistol. Afghan soldiers mostly used long *jezails* for long-distance shooting, and knives or swords for close-quarter fighting. However, contemporary prints show they sometimes also carried pistols, again for short-distance use. (Author's collection)

ABOVE RIGHT
The Afghan dagger was almost as feared as the *jezail*, and it was often used to finish off the wounded. The *chora*, known by the British as the 'Khyber Knife', had a razor-sharp, single-edged straight blade, used for slicing and cutting. This dagger was captured during the attack on Ghazni in 1839. (Image courtesy of the Somerset Military Museum Trust)

ORDERS OF BATTLE

BRITISH FORCES (ARMY OF THE INDUS)
Lieutenant-General Sir John Keane, commander-in-chief (from 6 April 1839)

BENGAL COLUMN (MAJOR-GENERAL SIR WILLOUGHBY COTTON) (2,430 CAVALRY, 5,570 INFANTRY, 31 GUNS)
Cavalry Brigade (Brigadier Arnold)
2nd Regiment Light Cavalry
HM 16th Lancers

3rd Regiment Light Cavalry
4th Regiment Local Horse
Detachment Skinner's, 1st Local Horse
Artillery (Brigadier Stevenson)
2nd Troop, 2nd Brigade Horse Artillery
4th Company, 2nd Battalion Foot
2nd Company, 6th Battalion Foot (camel battery)
Infantry Division
1st Infantry Brigade (Colonel Sale)
HM 13th Light Infantry
16th Regiment Native Infantry

48th Regiment Native Infantry

2nd Infantry Brigade (Major-General Nott)

31st Regiment Native Infantry

42nd Regiment Native Infantry

43rd Regiment Native Infantry

4th Infantry Brigade (Lieutenant-Colonel Roberts)

35th Regiment Native Infantry

37th Regiment Native Infantry

1st Bengal European Regiment

Two companies of sappers and miners

BOMBAY COLUMN (MAJOR-GENERAL WILLSHIRE) (1,200 CAVALRY, 4,280 INFANTRY, 24 GUNS)

Cavalry (Brigadier Scott)

Wing HM 4th Light Dragoons

1st Light Cavalry

Poona Local Horse

Artillery (Brigadier Stevenson)

3rd Troop, Horse Artillery

4th Troop Horse Artillery

Horse Field Battery

Infantry (Colonel Baumgardt)

HM 2nd Queens Royal Regiment of Foot

HM 17th Regiment of Foot

19th Regiment Native Infantry

Sappers and miners

SHAH SOOJAH'S FORCE (MAJOR-GENERAL SIMPSON) (950 CAVALRY, 5,000 INFANTRY, 12 GUNS)

1st Troop Horse Artillery

2nd Troop Horse Artillery

1st Regiment Cavalry

2nd Regiment Cavalry

1st Regiment Infantry

2nd Regiment Infantry

3rd Regiment Infantry

4th Regiment Light Infantry

5th Regiment Infantry

PRINCE TIMUR'S FORCE (SON OF SHAH SOOJAH) (LIEUTENANT-COLONEL WADE) (4,840 MEN)

Two companies, 20th Regiment Native Infantry

Two companies, 21st Regiment Native Infantry

400 Mahommedan Horse

600 irregulars cavalry

320 Juzzailchees

2,860 regular and irregular infantry

Two 24-pounder howitzers

Two 6-pounder guns

SIKH CONTINGENT (WITH PRINCE TIMUR'S FORCE) (COLONEL SHAIKH BUSSAWAN) (6,146 MEN)

Squadron of Cavalry

Irregular Missildars cavalry

Three battalions infantry

Two companies Poorubees infantry

Two battalions Nujeebs irregular infantry

One corps hill ranger irregular infantry

One battalion Ramgoles irregular infantry

Pioneers

One howitzer

One mortar

RESERVE FORCE AT FEROZEPUR (MAJOR-GENERAL DUNCAN) (4,250 MEN)

Cavalry

Skinner's Head Quarters Local Horse

Artillery

3rd Troop, 2nd Brigade Horse Artillery

3rd Company, 2nd Battalion Foot Artillery

Infantry

HM 3rd Regiment of Foot (the Buffs)

2nd Regiment Bengal Native Infantry

5th Regiment Bengal Native Infantry

20th Regiment Bengal Native Infantry

27th Regiment Bengal Native Infantry

53rd Regiment Bengal Native Infantry

BOMBAY RESERVE (SIND) (3,000 MEN) (BRIGADIER VALIANT) (3,000 MEN)

3rd Company, 1st Battalion Artillery

5th Company, Golundaze Batallion

HM 40th Regiment of Foot

2nd Regiment Bombay Native Infantry Grenadiers,

22nd Regiment Bombay Native Infantry

26th Regiment Bombay Native Infantry

AFGHAN FORCES

At the time of the British invasion, it was estimated by Mohan Lal, political assistant to Alexander Burnes, that Dost Mohammad had the following forces available to him:

50 pieces of cannon plus those captured from the Sikhs at Jamrud.

200 *Shahnaks* (camel artillery).

12,000 cavalry in two brigades: 9,000 *Khud Aspah* (riders with own horses) and 3,000 *Amala-yi sarkari* (riders with government horses) commanded by Dost Mohammad's sons.

2,000 *Jezailchis* (infantry with large muskets).

1,500 government infantry (commanded by Nayab Abdul Samad, Mr Cambell, and Dr Harlan).

OPPOSING PLANS

BRITISH PLANS

The Simla Manifesto, issued on 1 October 1838, provided the overall justification for the invasion and its general objectives: 'His Majesty Shah Soojah-oil-Mool will enter Afghanistan surrounded by his own troops, and will be supported against foreign interference and factious opposition by a British Army.' It was hoped that once the independence and integrity of Afghanistan under its new ruler was established, the British forces would be withdrawn. The continuing Persian siege of Herat was specifically mentioned in the Manifesto as an act of hostility towards Britain, as was the city of Kandahar whose chiefs (brothers of Dost Mohammad) were declared to be siding with the Persians in the full knowledge that this was against British interests. The clear implication was that both these cities would be military targets.

Before the army had been assembled, news came in September that the Persians had lifted the siege of Herat. The Afghans had mounted strong resistance, assisted by Eldred Pottinger, a young East India Company political officer who had originally trained in the artillery. However, more significantly for the Persians had been the British decision to send two ships and a battalion of infantry to the Kharak Island in the Persian Gulf as a warning of more intensive military action should they persist in their attack on Herat. The removal of the immediate threat to Herat, coupled with Russia withdrawing its support for further Persian aggression, undermined one of the core aims of the invasion. Nevertheless, Auckland still decided to proceed. However, given there was no longer any need to secure Herat, one division of the Bengal Column was to be sent back, and Sir Henry Fane withdrew from being commander of the army in favour of Sir John Keane. A new order from Lord Auckland was issued on 8 November. While he regarded the raising of the siege of Herat as a just cause of congratulation for the government of British India, nevertheless he would 'continue to prosecute with vigour the measures which have been announced with a view to the substitution of a friendly for a hostile power in the eastern provinces of Afghanistan, and for the establishment of a permanent barrier against schemes of aggressions upon our north-west frontier'.

The British plans were now based solely on regime change, and despite the arguments of Burnes, the opportunity to reopen negotiations with Dost Mohammad in the light of the changed circumstances was not taken. Auckland and his advisers still imagined that Shah Soojah would be welcomed as a legitimate ruler, and would be able to reunify Afghanistan in a way that

was still not possible for Dost Mohammad – Herat had remained under the control of Soojah's brother and there were continuing tribal tensions within the country. In any event, too many preparations were already in train with the mobilization of the army under way and, with winter approaching, any further delay would have meant forestalling the plans for another season. A dramatic reconsideration of the position of Dost Mohammad would have undermined the recently agreed tripartite treaty with Soojah and Ranjit Singh, and potentially only have created even greater uncertainties in the region. However, the strategy reflected a serious error in political intelligence and a lack of understanding of the realities of Afghan politics at the time. Sir John Kaye in his 1851 account of the war considered the invasion now to be simply an experiment, with more reasons why it should fail than why it should succeed: 'The expedition now to be undertaken had no longer any other ostensible object than the substitution of a monarch whom the people of Afghanistan had repeatedly, in emphatic, scriptural language, spued out, for those Barukzye chiefs who, whatever may have been the defect of their government, had contrived to maintain themselves in security, and their country in peace, with a vigour and constancy unknown to the luckless Suddozye Princes.'

AFGHAN PLANS

Lack of detailed written records makes it difficult to determine clear military plans of the Afghan opposition, but various contemporary accounts give an idea of the main strategic thinking. Dost Mohammad had attempted to professionalize a small proportion of his army, but he was still largely dependent on forces raised by tribal chiefs. Afghanistan could by no means be described as a unified state, but once the plans for invasion had been announced Dost Mohammad invoked Islam as a unifying force, and had a fatwa issued against Shah Soojah. Nevertheless, he was obliged to adopt a largely defensive strategy based on protecting the cities of Ghazni and Kabul in the eastern part of the country. With the Persians abandoning any designs on Herat, he was prepared to see the city – at least for the time being – continue under the governorship of its Sadozai ruler. Kandahar was not a military priority to defend, and in any event did not appear to be under immediate threat since Dost Mohammad initially thought that the main British force would enter through the Khyber Pass as the traditional route for invaders from the south. Unaware that the British had in fact taken the route through the Bolan Pass in the west, he sent his son, Akbar Khan, in command of the Afghan forces, to the Khyber Pass to resist the invasion. There, supported by local Pashtuns, he encountered the smaller force of 6,000 led by Shah Soojah's son, which was under the command of Colonel Wade, together with 6,000 Sikhs. Akbar Khan fell seriously ill – there were rumours he had been poisoned on the instigation of the British – and Wade was able to fight his way through the pass, losing 23 men with 158 wounded, and capture the garrison of Ali Masjid.

The British do not seem to have chosen the route to the Bolan Pass as a tactical ruse to mislead the Afghans. At 1,500 miles, it was three times the distance to Kabul than the more familiar route via Peshawar and the Khyber Pass, and the countryside was hardly known to the British. The main reason for adopting the route was the need to avoid offending Ranjit Singh who was clearly resistant to any idea of a large British military force crossing his territory. Once Dost Mohammad was aware of the direction being taken by the British, he employed delaying tactics by persuading tribes round the Bolan Pass and the nearby Khojak Pass to harass the British troops. He believed that the long lines of communication and difficulties in maintaining supplies between Kandahar and Kabul would weaken the British, and hoped to surround the British forces at Ghazni. Alternatively, there would be a major ambush of the British force in a narrow valley outside Kabul, with cavalry led by one of his sons cutting off the British from the rear.

His assessment of the challenges the British would face in trying to secure adequate supplies for such a large army in hostile territory was largely correct, and for much of the time the Army of the Indus was on half rations, and almost at starvation level. The unexpected death of Ranjit Singh in early 1839 caused further instability in the Punjab region and made the task of creating secure supply chains for the British Army even more challenging. Dost Mohammad's greatest difficulty, however, was ensuring loyalty amongst the different tribal factions, and instilling a real sense of national unity – it was his inability to do this that ultimately secured initial success for the invading British.

INVASION AND OCCUPATION, 1839–40

THE MARCH THROUGH THE BOLAN PASS

The Bengal Column, composed of over 8,000 fighting men, accompanied by some 38,000 camp followers, set off from Ferozepur on 10 December 1838 moving westwards towards the Indus River, with the aim of crossing into the Thar desert towards the Bolan Pass. The initial route was largely parallel with the Indus, and some hospital stores were sent by river, but not enough boats could be found to transport the main stores. An enormous number of animals were therefore needed. They moved slowly at around two miles per hour, and took up great distances – the marching army was some four miles in length. Around 500 bullocks and carts were used to transport supplies during the first stages, but the lack of adequate roads beyond the Indus meant that camels would have to be used as the main mode of supply transport. On leaving Ferozepur, some 15,000 camels were used to carry supplies only, but in reality this number almost doubled when private camels were added. Shortage of regular grazing for such large numbers meant that many camels had to be used to carry fodder for those camels carrying military supplies, while many individual officers seemed to be totally unaware of the supply demands that would lie ahead – one officer required no fewer than 60 camels for his personal belongings, while another regiment used two camels solely for carrying cigars.

Around 30 days' worth of supplies were sent with the army from Ferozepur together with enough cattle for slaughter for two and a half months. Some grain had been sent by river, but the advance planning, required to secure the supplies needed to sustain such a large force over a long distance in more remote country, seems to have been wholly inadequate, and this was

Map of the north-west frontier. The route travelled by the Army of the Indus was largely uncharted territory for the British, but the *Map of the North-Western Frontier of British India* produced by Jean-Baptiste Tassin and published by the Calcutta Oriental Lithographic Press in 1838 was a key resource for the military. (© Peter & Renate Nahum)

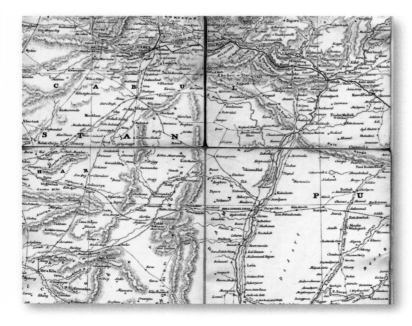

Route of the Army of the Indus, 1838–39

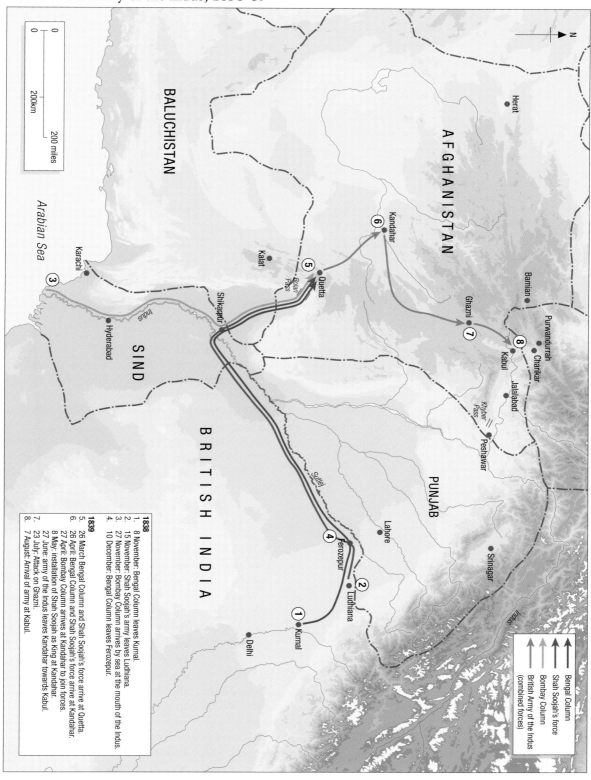

BALUCHISTAN

Arabian Sea

AFGHANISTAN

Herat

Kandahar ⑥

Kalat

⑤ Quetta

Bamian

Ghazni ⑦

Purwandurrah

Charikar

⑧ Kabul

Jalalabad

Khyber Pass

Peshawar

③ Karachi

Shikarpur

Indus

Hyderabad

SIND

Bolan Pass

B R I T I S H   I N D I A

PUNJAB

Sutlej

Lahore

Srinagar

Indus

④ Ferozepur

② Ludhiana

① Kurnal

Delhi

N

1838
1. 8 November: Bengal Column leaves Kurnal.
2. 15 November: Shah Soojah's army leaves Ludhiana.
3. 27 November: Bombay Column arrives by sea at the mouth of the Indus.
4. 10 December: Bengal Column leaves Ferozepur.

1839
5. 26 March Bengal Column and Shah Soojah's force arrive at Quetta.
6. 26 April: Bengal Column and Shah Soojah's force arrive at Kandahar.
7. 27 April: Bombay Column arrives at Kandahar to join forces.
8. 8 May: installation of Shah Soojah as King at Kandahar.
7. 27 June: army of the Indus leaves Kandahar towards Kabul.
8. 23 July: Attack on Ghazni.
8. 7 August: Arrival of army at Kabul.

Bengal Column
Shah Soojah's force
Bombay Column
British Army of the Indus (combined forces)

0
0

200km

200 miles

not helped by poor local harvests that year. The task of securing of supplies had been delegated to the East India Company political staff, a decision that the military bitterly regretted since it soon became clear they were not up to the challenge..

By the time the Bengal Column reached the Indus, crossing at Rohree on 24 January, 600 miles of marching over 70 days were taking their toll. An enormous number of camels had already died or were suffering, often being overloaded due to the lack of local forage. Many Indian camp followers who owned camels were unwilling to cross the Indus into unfamiliar and hostile territory, and simply left, taking their animals with them. Replacements bought from local breeding farms proved totally unsuitable for use as beasts of burden, horses were falling out of condition, and supplies of grain that were supposed to have been laid in were found to be wholly insufficient.

Engineers had gone a week ahead of the main column to construct a bridge of boats across the 500 yard width of river at Rohree, using an island in the middle as a break point. Around 74 large boats were used in all, and the operation took 20 days, being ready for crossing on 3 February. It was a major work of civil engineering carried out under difficult circumstances over fast-flowing waters, and the engineers later received special commendations from their commander-in-chief.

The Bengal Column together with camp followers crossed the bridge, and assembled at Shikarpore. The original intention had been to meet up here with the Bombay Column on its march from Karachi, under the overall command of General Keane, and then jointly march through the Bolan Pass. However, the Bombay Column had also faced difficulties with supplies and securing the cooperation of the Sind chieftains, and was at least a week behind. The British received news that local tribes, encouraged by Dost Mohammad, were now moving to block the Bolan Pass, and Macnaughten urged the commander of the Bengal Column, Sir Willoughby Cotton, not to wait for Keane but proceed at once to take possession of the pass.

The Bolan Pass. Dost Mohammad assumed the British invasion would follow the traditional route from India via the Khyber Pass. Instead, the main British force entered via the Bolan Pass towards the western side of the country. The road at the head of the pass was no more than 60ft wide with 100ft high perpendicular rocks on both sides. (National Army Museum)

The route to the head of the pass was some 150 miles, including some 30 miles of desert, and on 22 February, the Bengal Column set off carrying just 45 days' worth of supplies. It proved a terrible journey. Temperatures rose to 100 degrees Fahrenheit, and both soldiers and animals were obliged to travel at night. Tribesmen harassed the force, plundering straggling animals and baggage, local water supplies were contaminated, foraging on largely bare land proved insufficient, and many men fell ill with dysentery. Supplies had run so low that on 8 March, some 23 miles from the pass, non-combatants were put on half rations. They reached Dadur on 10 March, expecting to find at least ten days' worth of locally bought grain promised by the local chief. However, less than a tenth of the supplies needed were found, and after a week's rest, undernourished and exhausted, the army proceeded towards the Bolan Pass, climbing over 60 miles through sterile and stony ground, reaching the head of the pass five days later. There the road was at places no more than 60 feet wide, with over 100-foot high sheer rock faces on either side. Camels had to proceed slowly and reluctantly in single file, and conditions were so bad that towards the heights of the pass guns had to be dismantled and carried by hand. Apart from attacks on rear columns, there had so far been little in the way of sustained action from the Afghans, but at the head of the pass local tribesmen began harassing the army with sniper fire, and parties from the army were sent to dislodge them.

On 26 March, the army finally reached Quetta, which was described as 'a most miserable mud-town'. They had hoped to find plentiful supplies of grain, but once again they were to be thwarted – only one day's supply could be purchased locally, and rations were restricted even further with soldiers being put on half rations and camp followers on quarter rations. The offer of compensation by way of pay increases would have been scant reward for men in such a condition. Provisions still had somehow to be purchased, and regular orders were given that locals were not to be over harassed or forced to give over supplies for fear of antagonizing the population. Alexander Burnes led largely unproductive negotiations with Mehrab, the Khan of Kalat, who claimed that he was not in a position to force local grain merchants to sell supplies to the British. The British suspected duplicity since it was known that local merchants were willing to sell but pleaded they could not do so without the authority of Mehrab.

On 6 April, a 19-guns salute marked the arrival of Sir John Keane and Shah Soojah at Quetta. Sir John then took overall command of the Army of the Indus, and issued orders that sensibly included the joining of the Bengal and Bombay commissariats under a single command. The commissariats had been known to often compete with each other for the purchase of

Afghan snipers using accurate, long-range *jezails* had almost perfect defensive cover in the high rocks overlooking parts of the army's route. The only effective response to their attacks was to use crowning tactics to dislodge them from their positions. (© Peter & Renate Nahum)

supplies, leading to inflated costs and inefficiencies. Depots for ordinance and stores were to be established at Dadur and Quetta, and Major-General Nott was to remain with a rearguard at Quetta. Despite the desperate condition of the forces, the orders of the day put a brave face on the situation with Keane expressing 'his gratification at the proud position in which he is placed by the command of such fine troops'.

Keane, though, was a hard-nosed realist who would have realized the fraught position in which the army now found itself. Supplies were down to nine days, troops and camp followers were nearing starvation, and local tribesmen continued to carry out

The Khojak Pass. By the time the Army of the Indus reached the Khojak Pass on 14 April 1839, it was half starved through lack of provisions. Crossing the five-mile pass with its steep, narrow roads proved fatal for many of the camels, which slipped and fell into deep ravines. (Author's collection)

opportunistic attacks stealing cattle and camels. Communication to the rear was being cut off and large detachments would be required to deal with the problem – these could be ill afforded at this juncture. Sir Willoughby Cotton, who had resumed command of the 1st Division, was especially pessimistic at the prospect of continuing. Even Macnaughten, unimpressed with Cotton's despondency, wrote to Governor General Auckland on the same day stating: 'The fact is, the troops and followers are nearly in a state of mutiny for food.' Keane realized that adequate supplies of grain could not be secured from the Khan of Kalat, and that the only option was to proceed towards Kandahar, some 150 miles distant, the route to which involved another severe test, the Khojak Pass. Engineers were sent in advance to improve the road over the pass, and on 7 April the main force left Quetta. The Bombay Column was still some ten days behind, and was proceeding through the Bolan Pass, where they were faced with the sight of the remains of the numerous horses and camels that had perished during the crossing by the Bengal Column only weeks before.

KANDAHAR

On 12 April Sir John Keane and the head of the army reached the beginning of the Khojak Pass, the last major defile before the plains leading to Kandahar. For a force still on half rations, crossing the pass proved to be as challenging as the journey through the Bolan Pass. Many camels refused the steep ascent, and guns again had to be manhandled through the narrow defiles. Over 3,000 camels died during the crossing, and an enormous amount of baggage and supplies (including over 27,000 rounds of ammunition and 14 barrels of gunpowder) was abandoned.

The one comfort for the British was that the reported major opposing forces of Afghan tribes gathering in the pass failed to materialize. Kandahar chiefs had sent parties of horseman to observe the progress of the British,

For symbolic reasons Shah Soojah was assigned his own troops, numbering around 6,000, which included horse artillery, infantry, and cavalry, under the command of British officers. In this picture his artillery is crossing a river near Kandahar. (Anne S. K. Brown Military Collection, Brown University)

and while marauding bands continued to engage in the sporadic looting of animals and supplies, there were no sustained attacks. In truth, the British Army was physically far weaker than the Afghans probably realized, and a coordinated assault, focussed on the destruction of the animals rather than direct combat with troops, would have probably been sufficient to have forced the British to surrender or withdraw.

The army entered the plains leading towards Kandahar, which offered greater possibilities of local forage, though Keane still issued orders that growing crops must not be cut for fear of antagonizing the local populace. Kandahar chiefs had sent a body of around 2,000 cavalry to within 25 miles of the pass, but rather than engage they fell back towards the city as the British emerged. Luck began to change for the British when a local chieftain, Hajee Khan, aware of the failure of the Kandahar chiefs to fight, decided to switch sides and entered the British camp on 20 April to offer loyalty to Shah Soojah. Hajee Khan, notorious for double-dealing, was the first local chief to acknowledge Shah Soojah, and his action, together with an overestimation of the strength of the British Army (now down to just two days' worth of half rations and no grain for the horses) demoralized Dost Mohammad's half-brothers, who were then in control of Kandahar. No proper defences had been prepared, and shortly before the British arrived, the leaders and their families fled the city.

Shah Soojah was now permitted to lead his own force in advance of the main army towards Kandahar, symbolically showing his independent authority, and

Kandahar was an important city that fell to the British without resistance and provided much-needed provisions and a place for recuperation for the exhausted army. The British organized a coronation for Shah Soojah on the outskirts of the city. (National Army Museum)

he entered the city on 25 April. There was intense curiosity from the local inhabitants though it was doubtful whether this really amounted to 'feelings nearly amounting to adoration', as Macnaughten optimistically described Soojah's reception in a dispatch to Governor General Auckland. The main forces of the Bengal Column then arrived and were encamped on the outskirts of the city, shortly to be joined by the Bombay Column. At last, the opportunity was taken to refresh and replenish a half-starved force since local supplies of grain and other food were far more plentiful. Orders were issued to purchase horses to replenish the 500 horses (around 10 per cent of the total) that had died during the march. In all, the British remained at Kandahar for around two months. Some contemporary accounts criticize the decision not to pursue and capture the fleeing Kandahar chiefs, and the delay allowed Dost Mohammad more time to gather defences around Ghazni and Kabul. But Keane was probably correct in estimating that the force was simply not in a fit state for further military action, and that rest and recuperation was the order of the day, whatever immediate opportunities were lost as a result.

In the meantime, the decision was taken to mount a major ceremony on the outskirts of the city to mark the coronation of Shah Soojah. A Royal Salute was fired, and the combined Bengal and Bombay Columns were paraded in front of Shah Soojah. Macnaughten was delighted to see the first stage of his strategy come to fruition, but there were already signs that initial local support was waning. Plans were made on the expectation that several thousand local inhabitants would attend, but in reality only 100 or so left the city to watch the ceremony. The programme for the coronation had designated the area behind the throne for 'the populace restrained by the Shah's troops', an unintentionally ironic turn of phrase that did not go unnoticed by some of the British.

GHAZNI

Ghazni was the major fortress town on the road towards Kabul and was 229 miles from Kandahar. It was governed by one of Dost Mohammad's sons, and was planned by Dost Mohammad to be a vital part of his defence strategy. Although it was considered impregnable, he sent extra supplies for a possible long siege, and ordered the strengthening of the defences. Dost Mohammad still probably thought that the main immediate concern of the British force

The city of Ghazni blocked the route to Kabul, and was heavily defended by Afghan forces. Its high walls apparently made it impregnable, especially as the British had not brought adequate siege equipment with them. (© Peter & Renate Nahum)

at Kandahar would be to first secure Herat in the west – news that the Persians had withdrawn had not yet reached him. The long stay of the army at Kandahar may have suggested this was indeed the British intention, and that any advance on Kabul was likely to wait another season giving Dost Mohammad more time to raise a large enough army for resistance. An initial strike on Herat might indeed have been required, for the British received intelligence from its political agents in the city that although the Persians had lifted the siege, the Sadozai governor of the city was now flirting with the Persians to support an attack against the British and his own brother Shah Soojah. The Persians declined the offer to be involved, and the governor then offered allegiance to Shah Soojah, and a British mission was sent from Kandahar to negotiate a treaty of friendship.

If the British did march eastwards towards Ghazni, Dost Mohammad considered that they would simply bypass the city rather than risk a difficult siege, and carry on the 90 miles to Kabul. If, on the other hand, they did carry out a conventional siege, this would add further delays, providing more time for the strengthening of Kabul's defences. He sent his eldest son, Afzal Khan, with a detachment of 3,000 cavalry to wait in the hills near Ghazni, while he amassed larger forces near Kabul. The plan was to ambush the advancing British force in a narrow valley on the outskirts of Kabul, with Afzal Khan's cavalry trapping and attacking the British from the rear.

Keane felt he had little option but to set off towards Kabul with the main forces of the Bengal and Bombay Columns together with Shah Soojah's forces, while General Nott was called upon to maintain a smaller force in Kandahar to be used as a base for securing communication lines back through the Bolan Pass and India. The march towards Ghazni was far less treacherous than the mountainous routes to Kandahar, and Keane and an advance party of engineers reached the outskirts of Ghazni on 22 July, where they proceeded to reconnoitre the city from nearby hills. Shah Soojah was urging the British to avoid confrontation and continue the march on to Kabul, but to leave such a strong fortress in the enemy hands to the rear would have been a high-level risk. Keane also calculated that the British forces had at the most three days' provisions left, making any immediate advance on Kabul impossible.

Captain George Thomson was the chief engineer to the Army of the Indus. He advised General Keane that in the absence of siege equipment the only feasible way to take Ghazni was to blow open one of the gates using gunpowder. He returned to India to resume command of the Bengal Sappers and Miners, and was promoted to lieutenant-colonel in 1854. (Image courtesy of Major R. D. Langrishe)

The attack on Ghazni,

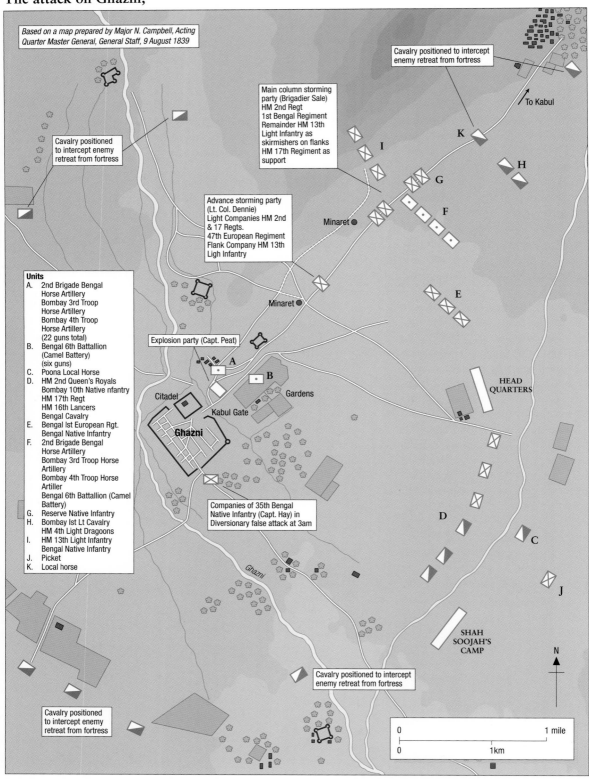

Based on a map prepared by Major N. Campbell, Acting Quarter Master General, General Staff, 9 August 1839

Cavalry positioned to intercept enemy retreat from fortress

To Kabul

Cavalry positioned to intercept enemy retreat from fortress

Main column storming party (Brigadier Sale)
HM 2nd Regt
1st Bengal Regiment
Remainder HM 13th Light Infantry as skirmishers on flanks
HM 17th Regiment as support

Advance storming party (Lt. Col. Dennie)
Light Companies HM 2nd & 17 Regts.
47th European Regiment
Flank Company HM 13th Ligh Infantry

Minaret

Minaret

Units

A. 2nd Brigade Bengal Horse Artillery
Bombay 3rd Troop Horse Artillery
Bombay 4th Troop Horse Artillery
(22 guns total)
B. Bengal 6th Battallion (Camel Battery) (six guns)
C. Poona Local Horse
D. HM 2nd Queen's Royals
Bombay 10th Native nfantry
HM 17th Regt
HM 16th Lancers
Bengal Cavalry
E. Bengal Ist European Rgt.
Bengal Native Infantry
F. 2nd Brigade Bengal Horse Artillery
Bombay 3rd Troop Horse Artillery
Bombay 4th Troop Horse Artiller
Bengal 6th Battallion (Camel Battery)
G. Reserve Native Infantry
H. Bombay Ist Lt Cavalry
HM 4th Light Dragoons
I. HM 13th Light Infantry
Bengal Native Infantry
J. Picket
K. Local horse

Explosion party (Capt. Peat)

Citadel

Ghazni

Kabul Gate

Gardens

HEAD QUARTERS

Companies of 35th Bengal Native Infantry (Capt. Hay) in Diversionary false attack at 3am

Ghazni

SHAH SOOJAH'S CAMP

Cavalry positioned to intercept enemy retreat from fortress

Cavalry positioned to intercept enemy retreat from fortress

N

0   1 mile

0   1km

As the entrances to Ghazni had been heavily strengthened with masonry, and with walls over 60 feet high surrounded by ditches, a conventional attack using mines and ladders was not feasible. The four heavy siege guns, which had been so laboriously manhandled through the passes, had been left behind in Kandahar, a decision that Keane bitterly regretted. The reasons for this failure are not easily explained, but may have been due to poor intelligence about the strength of the fortifications, and over-optimistic reports that, as with Kandahar, no defence would be offered. The army did possess a small battering ram but this had also been left in Kandahar due to a lack of transport cattle, though the chief engineer in any event doubted it would have been large enough to cope with the massive Ghazni walls. Luck was once again with the British when a disaffected nephew of Dost Mohammad offered allegiance to Shah Soojah. He had recently been inside the city and provided fresh intelligence on the state of

Advance into Ghazni. As soon as the gates were blown, the advance party and the storming party under Brigadier Sale entered the gates. Initially, there was considerable confusion because there was so much rubble and debris following the explosion. (Anne S. K. Brown Military Collection, Brown University. Image courtesy of Major R. D. Langrishe)

ATTACK ON GHAZNI, 23 JULY 1839 (PP. 44–45)

Ghazni was a fortress town situated on the route between Kandahar and Kabul. With walls over 60ft high (**1**), surrounded by ditches, and containing an imposing citadel (**2**), it was considered impregnable. Shah Soojah urged Sir John Keane, commander of the Army of the Indus, to bypass the fort and continue towards Kabul, but this would have been far too risky a strategy. Siege guns had been left behind in Kandahar, and the chief engineer, Thomson, advised that the city's defences made conventional techniques of mining and escalading impossible. The gates to the city had been blocked with stones and rubble, but intelligence was received that one gate, the Kabul Gateway (**3**), had been left untouched to allow communication with Kabul. Thomson recommended a *coup de main* – since the bridge over the ditch was unbroken (**4**) and the road up to the gate clear, it could be possible to blow the gate with gunpowder under cover, and storm the fortress by surprise. In the early morning of the 23rd a small group of engineers – three officers, three sergeants, and 18 sappers – approached the gate and laid some 300 pounds of gunpowder in 12 sandbags. The operation was designed to be conducted in silence and in secret, but they were challenged, and the Afghans began firing from the walls (**5**). Contemporary accounts refer to blue lights (**6**), some form of illumination flare, glaring from the top of the battlements. Lieutenant Durand, one of the officers, recounted afterwards: 'The sappers, having

deposited the last of the powder and retired. Durand, aided by Sergeant Robertson, uncoiled the hose, laying it close to the foot of the scarp, whilst the defenders, impatient at the restraint of their loopholes, jumped up at the top of their parapets, and poured their fire at the foot of the wall, hurling down also lumps of earth, stones, and bricks, but omitting fortunately the blue lights.' The 70-foot linen hose was laid out, fortuitously reaching a previously unknown sallyport which provided some shelter for the engineers. For a time, it proved impossible to light using a slow match but eventually it caught, and the engineers retired (**7**) to avoid the explosion. There remained some confusion as to whether the gate had been fully destroyed but eventually a bugler sounded the attack. The advance party (**8**) of four companies (HM 2nd and 17th regiments, 1st Bengal Infantry, and a flank company of HM 13th Light Infantry) under the command of Lieutenant-Colonel Dennie (**9**) that had been waiting at the bridge, now moved to enter the gateway, closely supported by a larger storming party commanded by Brigadier Sale. After three hours of fierce street fighting, the city was taken by the British with just 17 killed on their side, and the Afghans sustaining losses of over a thousand. The fall of Ghazni utterly demoralized Dost Mohammad who abandoned Kabul allowing the British to enter the city without resistance.

the defences, informing the British that one gate, the Kabul Gate, had not been strengthened with masonry in order to keep it open for communications with Kabul, and could be susceptible to mining with gunpowder. Although a risky operation, on the advice of the chief engineer, Keane took the decision that this was the only feasible way of breaching the city.

The main army was moved towards the Kabul road to cut off communications, and in the early morning of the 23rd, under the cover of darkness, a small group of sappers approached the Kabul Gate. They were accompanied by an advance guard of four companies of infantry while the main storming force of European infantry, under the command of Brigadier Sale, moved into position. A wing of native infantry was moved towards the gardens on the eastern side of the city to provide a false attack as a diversion to distract the enemy. Surprise was a key to success, and the complex set of orders issued by Keane emphasised that all movement must be made without the sound of bugle or trumpet. The firing of British guns from the hills overlooking the city provided a further distraction, though they were largely harmless given their size. With dawn just breaking, the sappers approached the gate, but they were challenged, and the Afghans began a raking fire from the upper ramparts. This proved ineffective because of the angles of fire, but inexplicably they failed to shoot from the lower works, from where they could probably have annihilated the small British contingent. The powder was laid, but there continued to be delays when the 70-foot fuse would not light, raising concerns among the storming party that the operation had failed.

Eventually, the powder was lit and the gate blown. Even then there was considerable confusion, with Brigadier Sale at one point assuming that a retreat should be ordered because of the difficulties of advancing through the rubble. By this point, all thought of surprise was out of the question, and the advance guard led by Captain Dennie met with fierce hand-to-hand resistance from Afghans at the entrance to the broken gateway. Sale still held back but a bugler decided, against orders, to sound the attack, and the main storming party advanced into the city. Over three hours of close fighting in narrow streets and passages then ensued, before a British flag was raised. The Afghans suffered severe casualties with some 1,200 killed and 1,800 taken prisoner, including the Governor, while the British suffered just 17 dead and 165 wounded.

There was over three hours of fierce fighting in Ghazni's narrow streets, with the Afghans firing from the ramparts, roofs of houses, and the citadel. However, as soon as the colours of the HM 13th Light Infantry and HM 17th were seen flying from the top fort, resistance collapsed. (Anne S. K. Brown Military Collection, Brown University)

DOST MOHAMMAD'S RETREAT

The sudden fall of Ghazni may have been achieved by a mixture of luck and bravery on the British side, but it changed the whole military situation. Much needed supplies of horses, camels and food were found within the city, and Dost Mohammad's son, Afzal Khan, in command of the reserve force of 3,000 Afghan cavalry, had retreated towards Kabul on seeing the British flag flying in the city. Dost Mohammad himself was facing a major rebellion from chieftains in Kohistan, possibly encouraged by the British, and ordered his son Akbar Khan to abandon any defence of the Khyber Pass and return to Kabul with the major part of the Afghan army. This retreat allowed the small British force entering the Khyber Pass under the nominal command of Shah Soojah's son to reach Jalalabad.

Dost Mohammad still envisaged a major battle at Arghandeh, ten miles west of Kabul where the narrow valley and deep gullies would have offered ideal terrain to ambush the British with devastating effect. With Akbar Khan's arrival he had some 13,000 fighting men, but it became increasingly clear that he could not count on the loyalty of local chieftains, many of whom had now begun to switch allegiance to Shah Soojah. Dost Mohammad, no longer convinced that his military strategy could succeed, then tried to make political overtures to the British, possibly imagining a scenario where he could retain control of the eastern parts of Afghanistan, leaving Shah Soojah with the cities of Kandahar, Herat and the western part of the country. One of his brothers was sent to discuss terms, including proposals that Shah Soojah be accepted as king with Dost Mohammad resuming the traditional Barokzai role of *wazir*, or chief minister. The British firmly rejected the overture, and Dost Mohammad and his family fled to the north towards Bokhara, pursued unsuccessfully by a small British detachment.

THE OCCUPATION OF KABUL

Leaving a small garrison at Ghazni, Keane and the main army proceeded to an undefended Kabul, arriving there on 7 August. As at Kandahar, Shah Soojah was symbolically permitted to lead the entry into the city, leaving the main British forces encamped on the outskirts. There was no resistance, but equally no great enthusiasm from the inhabitants.

With Shah Soojah installed on his own throne in the royal place, the British faced two main options. The invasion had achieved its core objectives and despite the appalling supply problems along the route, the cost, in terms of soldier lives lost, had been minimal, though causalities among the camp followers had been far higher, and there had been a heavy loss of animals. According to the terms of the Simla Manifesto, 'when once secured in power, and the independence and integrity of Afghanistan established, the British army will be withdrawn.' The qualification, 'when once secured in power', had been carefully drafted in rather ambiguous terms, and was not necessarily satisfied as soon as Shah Soojah was enthroned in Kabul. One option could have been to leave Shah Soojah at this point on the grounds that this would give him the opportunity to create an effective civil administration and secure the loyalty of his subjects, something he might have more easily achieved without the presence of a foreign army supporting him. Shah Soojah was not

The British forces encamped outside Kabul. When the British first arrived at Kabul they encamped in tents outside the city, but moved to temporary quarters in the Bala Hissar during the winter months. It soon became clear that a large force would have to remain for some time, and plans were made to build more permanent cantonments outside the city, a decision that would later prove disastrous. (New York Public Library)

politically naive, and against the advice of some of his Sadozai advisers was already offering a hand of friendship to the Barakzais.

Despite Macnaughten's continuing belief that Shah Soojah was the legitimate ruler, he was reluctant to withdraw the British forces at this point, especially as intelligence reports advised that Russian forces were advancing on Khiva again raising concerns about the threat of a Russian invasion. Sir John Keane was sanguine about the reality of any Russian threats, but Macnaughten advised Governor General Auckland that, while some of the army should return, a large force would have to remain in occupation for the time being to support

The entry of Shah Soojah into Kabul. On 7 August 1839, Shah Soojah entered the city of Kabul while the main British force remained encamped outside the city. Large crowds came out to see his return but their only show of enthusiasm was to stand up as he went by, and sit down again once he had passed. (Anne S. K. Brown Military Collection, Brown University)

49

Shah Soojah and deter any threats from Russia. Auckland himself had carefully considered the situation and saw the advantages of withdrawing the army back to India, both economic and military, particularly given the uncertain situation in the Punjab following Ranjit Singh's death. However, he concluded that the risk was too great for a complete immediate withdrawal and that a brigade of British troops should remain until the situation became clearer.

On 18 September 1839, the Bombay Column under General Willshire left the city to return to India via the Bolan Pass. A month later, Sir John Keane departed taking the route back via the Khyber Pass, remarking to an officer accompanying him that he should be congratulated on quitting Afghanistan at this point 'for mark my words, it will not be long before there is here some signal catastrophe'. There were indeed already ominous signs that all was not well. Dost Mohammad was still at large in the north, and apparently planning resistance. The Russian threat, however unrealistic, remained alive, and the Persians seemed to be once again turning their sights on Herat. On top of all these concerns, it became increasingly clear that support for Shah Soojah was not nearly as extensive as Macnaughten had hoped. The original plans to leave just a brigade were revised, and Macnaughten persuaded Keane to depart with only a small contingent leaving behind the bulk of the Bengal Column under the command of Sir Willoughby Cotton.

THE BRITISH INSTALLATION AT KABUL

Kabul Bazaar. The main bazaars in the city of Kabul were a delight to the British following the hardships of the invasion. They were full of exotic fruits and other foodstuffs, and according to a contemporary account they sold articles and goods of all kinds from almost every part of the world including England, Russia, and India. (Author's collection)

It was now clear that the sizeable British force would remain much longer in Kabul than originally intended, but just how long remained unknown. The British Foreign Secretary, Palmerston, hoped the British could help Shah Soojah train up a professional Afghan army that would provide sufficient security to allow a complete British departure, but this could take years rather than months. The British Army on arrival at Kabul had originally been installed in tents on the outskirts, but more permanent arrangements now needed to be made. The military advice was that the obvious location for accommodating the British was within the Bala Hissar, the fortress area of Kabul overlooking the city, and the troops had been lodged there during the winter. Shah Soojah, who occupied the royal palace within the Bala Hissar, was clearly uncomfortable with the prospect of sharing his quarters with foreign troops, not least because of the poor image it would present for someone claiming the political legitimacy of his position. He persuaded Macnaughten that another location would have to be found.

Various forts on the outskirts of the city had been considered, but eventually land some two miles from the walls of Kabul was chosen. The political considerations of maintaining good relations with

View of the city of Kabul from the Bala Hissar. It would have made more military sense for the British forces to have remained within the Bala Hissar overlooking the city. However, the British cantonments were built in a vulnerable position on open land towards the Beymaru Heights, which can be seen in the background of the picture towards the right. (Private collection)

Shah Soojah were the main reason for the location, and in any event Governor General Auckland had already turned down requests to improve the physical strength of the Bala Hissar on economic grounds. It may have also been thought that any offensive action would take place in other parts of the country. Certainly, as a defensive position should an insurrection taken place, the location for the cantonments was disastrous, and Lieutenant Eyre, in charge of ordinance in Kabul, noted witheringly that, in defiance of all rule and precedent, 'the position eventually fixed upon for our magazine and cantonment was a piece of swampy ground, commanded on all sides by hills or forts'.

The location may have been bad, but worse still the construction of the cantonments appeared to take little note of the possibility of ever having to defend it against attack. A square of around 1,000 yards in length and 600 yards wide, parallel with the main Kohistan road, housed the main body of the troops. It was surrounded by a small wall and ditch, with bastions at each corner, but these were overlooked by the surrounding hills. A further square, about half the size and surrounded by a smaller wall, was attached at one end. It would be known as the Mission Compound, half to be used for a house for Macnaughten and the other half for buildings for the other officers. The compound's casual and exposed attachment to the main cantonments

Gate to the Bala Hissar. Taken during the Second Afghan War (1878–80) this photograph of the main gate to the Bala Hissar gives a feel of how impressive the citadel would have been during its prime. (© Peter & Renate Nahum)

Beymaru Heights and the cantonments. The Beymaru Heights provided a commanding position over the poorly sited British cantonments at Kabul. This contemporary drawing is the only one that gives a good impression of the size and layout of the cantonments. Officers' quarters were in the two-storey buildings. (Art and Architecture Collection, Miriam and Ira D. Wallach Division of Art, Prints and Photographs, The New York Public Library, Astor, Lenox and Tilden Foundations)

only increased its vulnerability. An even worse decision was taken to place the main commissariat in an old fortress about half a mile away on the road towards the city – this location would prove fatal during the uprising 18 months later. The whole area of land between the cantonments and the city was dotted with small forts, and ditches.

Many of the military could see the vulnerability of both the position of the cantonments and their construction. Macnaughten appears to have been the key decision maker, and in response to any criticisms during construction, Lieutenant Sturt, the officer in charge of design, noted that he had submitted plans to Macnaughten, and hearing nothing had assumed all was in order. One would have thought that the final say for operational decisions of such significance should clearly have rested with the military, but Macnaughten's relationship, as Political Agent, with the military command was always less than clear. The decision was then taken to split the military command, which only strengthened Macnaughten's overall position. General Nott was to remain in Kandahar with responsibility for keeping open the lines of communication through the Bolan Pass, while General Cotton, based in Kabul, was responsible for the more challenging Northern Command operating in often unstable and hostile territory. Small garrisons were spread out in a number of locations, a penny-packet tactic heavily criticized by Brigadier Roberts, then in command of Shah Soojah's troops, since troops would be extremely vulnerable should local tribes turn hostile and cut off communications. The disposition of the troops outside Kabul in the Northern Command was, therefore, as follows:

Disposition of British Forces, 1839

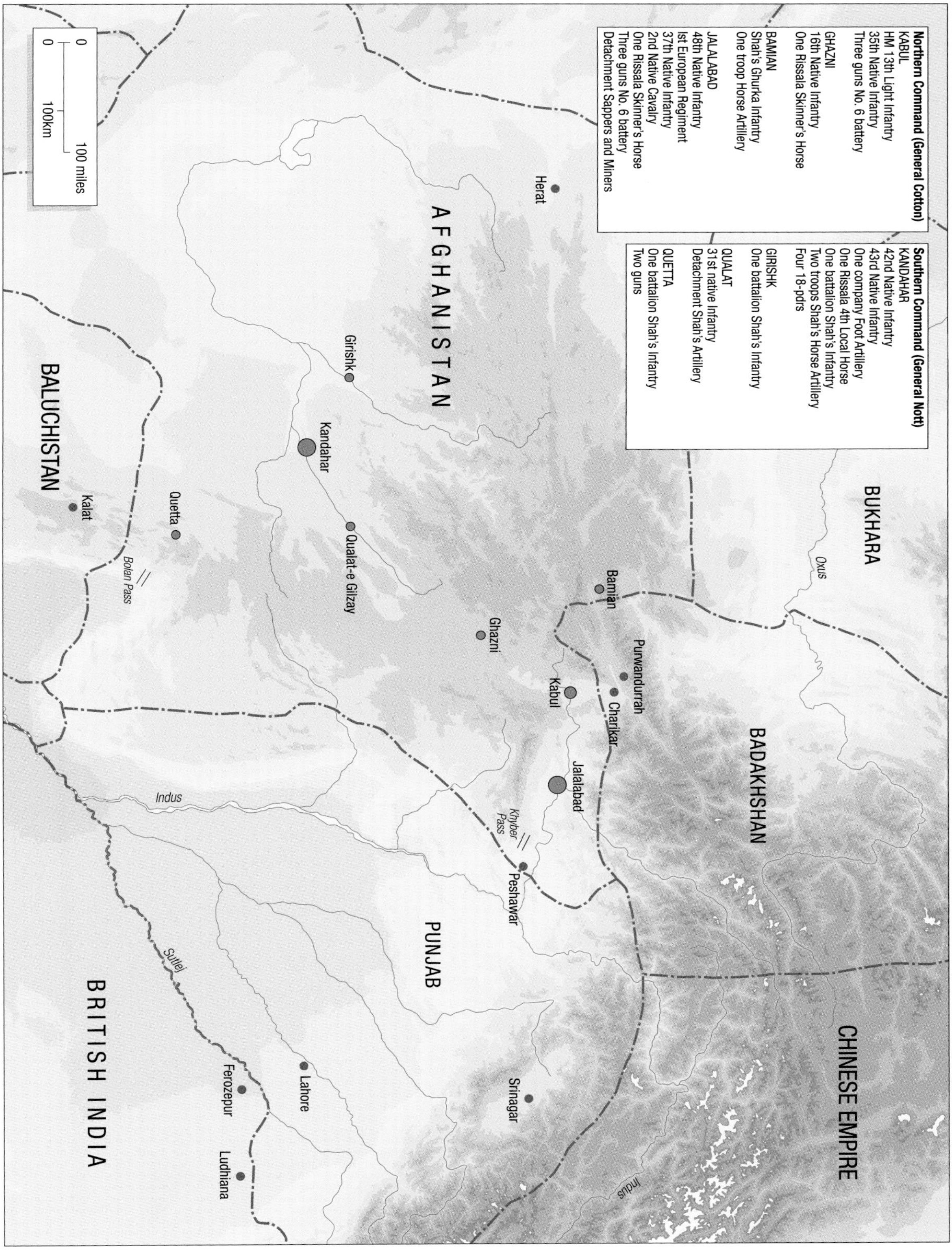

Northern Command (General Cotton)

KABUL
HM 13th Light Infantry
35th Native Infantry
Three guns No. 6 battery

GHAZNI
16th Native Infantry
One Rissala Skinner's Horse

BAMIAN
Shah's Ghurka Infantry
One troop Horse Artillery

JALALABAD
48th Native Infantry
1st European Regiment
37th Native Infantry
2nd Native Cavalry
One Rissala Skinner's Horse
Three guns No. 6 battery
Detachment Sappers and Miners

Southern Command (General Nott)

KANDAHAR
42nd Native Infantry
43rd Native Infantry
One company Foot Artillery
One Rissala 4th Local Horse
One battalion Shah's Infantry
Two troops Shah's Horse Artillery
Four 18-pdrs

GIRISHK
One battalion Shah's Infantry

QUALAT
31st native Infantry
Detachment Shah's Artillery

QUETTA
One battalion Shah's Infantry
Two guns

AFGHANISTAN

BALUCHISTAN

BUKHARA

BADAKHSHAN

CHINESE EMPIRE

PUNJAB

BRITISH INDIA

Herat

Girishk

Kandahar

Kalat

Quetta

Qualat-e Gilzay

Bamian

Ghazni

Purwandurrah

Kabul

Charikar

Jalalabad

Peshawar

Srinagar

Lahore

Ferozepur

Ludhiana

Oxus

Indus

Indus

Sutlej

Bolan Pass

Khyber Pass

0 _____ 100 miles
0 _____ 100km

DOST MOHAMMAD'S FIGHTBACK AND SURRENDER

In September 1840, Dost Mohammad made one last attempt to mount a campaign of major resistance to the British. A virtual prisoner in Bokhara, he had escaped and rallied forces in the north, playing on the disaffections of the Kohistanis with the new regime's imposition of levies. Together with some 6,000 Uzbek cavalry, he began to move towards Kabul. The British had already sent a series of small detachments that had engaged successfully with the Afghans, but Dost Mohammad kept eluding capture. A larger force under General Sale, including some 2,000 infantry, was then sent, and confronted Dost Mohammad at Parwan, only 60 miles north of Kabul. The British felt an easy victory was in the offing, but an advance party of two squadrons of the 2nd Bengal Lancers were overwhelmed by an Afghan cavalry charge. Sale, concerned that the remaining forces could be surrounded in difficult countryside, retreated back to Kabul.

Dost Mohammad seemed to have underestimated the very real alarm his victory had caused to the British, confirming Macnaughten's worst fears that a major revolt was now in play. Some Afghan historians consider that Dost Mohammad now failed to capitalize on his position and that an uprising of a genuinely united national force was within in his grasp. Certainly, an immediate large-scale assault on Kabul might well have persuaded the British to leave. However, Dost Mohammad was less than sure of the loyalty of the various tribes to his cause, and disappeared from the scene of victory. The next day he turned up alone in Kabul to offer his surrender to Macnaughten

The surrender of Dost Mohammad. In 1840, Dost Mohammad mounted a spirited resistance against the British who had deposed him the previous year. However, uncertain of the loyalty of tribal leaders, on 3 November he decided to surrender to Macnaughten outside the city walls of Kabul. He was treated with courtesy and exiled to India. (Author's collection)

where he was treated with courtesy and respect, with Macnaughten even writing, 'He is certainly a wonderful fellow,' and refusing Shah Soojah's request to hand over the prisoner for execution. Ten days later Dost Mohammad was sent under escort to exile back in India to join his family, though his son, Akbar Khan, remained at large.

Dost Mohammad's surrender appeared to usher in a period of peace, though this was owed more to the British paying extensive bribes to local tribes than any widespread acceptance of Shah Soojah's regime. Life in the cantonments began to resemble the domestic colonial atmosphere in India. Officers' wives, and children, were permitted to join their husbands, and horse racing, cricket, skating, tending gardens for growing vegetables, and amateur theatricals became the order of the day.

During the war there was often a mutual attraction between British soldiers and Afghan women, including at least one marriage. However, fraternization and the dishonour it was thought to bring was one of the causes of the initial riots in Kabul in November 1841. (© Peter & Renate Nahum)

The Durbah-Khaneh of Shah Soojah in Kabul. There was relative peace in Kabul for most of 1841. Shah Soojah held a daily assembly of his senior officials and tribal leaders in the reception hall within the lower part of the Bala Hissar fortress. Shah Soojah is seen seated on his throne on the balcony. (Private collection)

THE RISING, 1841

SIGNS OF UNREST OUTSIDE KABUL

Despite the apparent peace, seeds were being sown that would lead to major insurrection in Kabul, and the eventual capitulation of the British forces. Sir Willoughby Cotton had retired, and Auckland replaced him with General Elphinstone rather than General Nott who was the abler soldier and already in the country. It was another sign of how King's officers were favoured over those from the East India Company, and Elphinstone, already a sick man in retirement, initially tried to refuse. However, Auckland may have thought that a dynamic military commander was no longer necessary given the apparent peacefulness of the situation – Macnaughten had recently written to him: 'All things considered, the perfect tranquillity of the country is to my mind perfectly miraculous.' On arrival at Kabul, Elphinstone immediately saw the vulnerability of the cantonments and offered to have them strengthened at his own expense, but this offer was rejected by Macnaughten. Elphinstone's position was not helped by the appointment of Brigadier Shelton as his second-in-command. An intemperate officer, he despised Elphinstone's lack of capability, and made no secret about it.

Macnaughten himself was already being urged by Auckland and the East India Company's Board of Directors to reduce costs, and had sought to cut the levies being paid to Afghan chiefs. The inability of the British to refrain from involving themselves in what might have been considered matters of internal administration only helped to confuse lines of authority and demarcation, undermining Shah Soojah's own position and his relationship with his subjects. The pressure on Macnaughten was made worse by the new Tory administration that had come to power back in England. It was far less enamoured of the whole Afghan venture than the previous government, and intent on further economic cutbacks. Macnaughten's strategy of increasing the professionalism of the Shah's army only exacerbated the situation as it deprived local chiefs of their traditional source of revenue, the raising of troops for Afghan rulers in return for land or money. Now levies were now being imposed directly to pay for increasing the Shah's forces, and the task of administrating the new system had been transferred to the British to ensure greater efficiency. Many tribal leaders were left feeling that there was unfair treatment between different tribes.

The first sign of the real problems this would raise was the cutting in half of subsidies being paid to the Ghilzai tribes guarding the Khyber Pass.

General Sale was sent with a brigade to secure the route, but found the Ghilzais in a state of insurrection, and was forced back to the village of Gandamak. Communications back to Kabul were being cut off, and trouble was brewing in Kohistan and among some of the Durrani tribes.

The vulnerability of the British military position was rapidly becoming apparent. There were brigades at Kandahar (under Nott), Jalalabad, (under Sale), and Kabul (under Elphinstone) but smaller detachments could hardly move in hostile territory, and the small 'penny-packet' garrisons scattered round the country had little defence. On 2 November, 130 soldiers marching from Kandahar to Kabul were attacked near Ghazni and took refuge in a fort at Syadabad, apparently under the protection of a friendly tribal leader. However, they were besieged, and the total force was destroyed.

On 3 November, a large force of Kohistani tribesmen attacked the fortified residence of Lugmani where Eldred Pottinger was resident, and cut off communications to Kabul, only 40 miles to the south. A detachment of 200 Ghurkhas in Shah Soojah's 4th Regiment based at Charikar some three miles away unsuccessfully tried to relieve the residence, and were forced to retire back to Charikar. There the total force of 740 was surrounded and besieged for over a week, with low supplies of food and ammunition, and nearly half were killed or wounded. The decision was taken to evacuate back to Kabul but by then complete confusion reigned, and the remaining soldiers were killed or captured. Only Pottinger and four others managed to reach Kabul on 15 November.

On 20 November, Ghazni, under command of Colonel Palmer and the 27th Bengal Native Infantry, was besieged by a force led by a nephew of Akbar Khan. News that a large force of reinforcements, on its way to assist the forces in Kabul, had been sent from Kandahar lead to a temporary cessation of the siege. However, when it became clear the reinforcements had been forced to return to Kandahar due to the adverse weather conditions, hostilities resumed. The city was overwhelmed on 7 December, and the garrison had to withdraw to the citadel. They remained there under siege for a month but, with food and with ammunition running out, agreed a truce on 15 January 1842, on the promise of safe withdrawal to Peshawar. However, on leaving the citadel they were attacked, and most of the sepoys were killed or captured. The British officers were taken prisoner, and in August the nine survivors were taken to Kabul as hostages.

General Sir Robert Sale. Commanding the 13th Light Infantry, Colonel (later General) Sale had led the storming party at Ghazni, showing characteristic bravery in hand-to-hand combat. Known as 'Fighting Bob', he later found himself unable to clear the Khyber Pass and was trapped in Jalalabad, unable to provide assistance to the British forces in Kabul. (Image courtesy of the Somerset Military Museum Trust)

THE INSURRECTION IN KABUL AND THE BRITISH RESPONSE

It is possible that Macnaughten failed to give sufficient attention to these ominous signs of discontent among a number of important tribes as he was about to return to India to take up the governorship of Bombay, with Alexander Burnes assuming the role of Envoy in Kabul. Elphinstone's continued ill health meant that he too was to return to India, with General Nott lined up to take his place. Nott had already proved himself militarily adept at handling local insurrections around Kandahar, and would no doubt have made a robust and decisive response to the disturbances that were about to take place in Kabul. Had the initial insurrections in Kabul in November taken place just two weeks later when Nott was due to assume command, it is likely that there would have been a very different outcome, though it would not have been one that would have dealt with the longer-term challenges of the occupation. There was no indication that the initial disturbances were in any way a coordinated attack on the British – it was the apparent failure of the British to take effective and immediate responsive action that allowed the Afghans, over the next six weeks, to increase their numbers, and mount a major attack, eventually forcing the British force to agree withdrawal terms.

2 November

The problems started on 2 November when reports reached the cantonments that Burnes' house within the city had been attacked at dawn by a mob of around 300 Afghans. They were partly motivated by dissatisfaction with the way the British had been distributing levies to different tribes, as some tribes were perceived to have been unfairly favoured over others. However, there was also growing anger at the sense of dishonour caused by the British indulging in excessive fraternization with local women, and by many accounts, Burnes himself was one of the worst offenders. Burnes tried to calm down the crowd, but was killed and the nearby house holding the British treasury, which was used to pay Shah Soojah's army, was looted.

To the despair of many in the cantonments, Elphinstone rejected any immediate British military response. He was conscious that that it might lead to a large loss of life in the narrow streets of the city, and assumed what was happening was a relatively minor disturbance rather than the start of a major uprising.

In any event, Shah Soojah was reluctant to see British troops fighting within his own city. Instead, he sent his own troops to quell the riot, but they were unsuccessful, losing some 200 and retreating back to the Bala Hissar. At the time a number of British troops under the command of Brigadier Shelton were encamped on the Seeah Sung hills overlooking the cantonments. Shelton was ordered to send a detachment to assist

The murder of Alexander Burnes. On 2 November 1841 the insurrection in Kabul started when a large crowd gathered outside the house of Alexander Burnes, the second most senior political officer in Kabul. Burnes unsuccessfully tried to calm the crowd down, and was murdered with his younger brother while trying to escape in local disguise. (Anne S. K. Brown Military Collection, Brown University)

Shah Soojah but had been given imprecise orders, being told simply to act according to his own judgment. This took the form of the fairly ineffective firing of guns from the Bala Hissar down onto the city. Meanwhile, the rest of the troops stationed at Seeah Sung were ordered back into the cantonments and the 37th Native Infantry was ordered back from Khord Kabul.

3 November

The 37th Native Infantry arrived and further reinforcements were sent to the Bala Hissar, including extra guns. Shah Soojah was now effectively holed up in the fortress with Shelton's troops while the city succumbed to mob rule. Increasing numbers of tribesmen were joining what was becoming far more serious than a localized riot, and, with their numbers estimated to be around 5,000, their attention was turning towards the cantonments. A detachment of one company of HM 44th Foot (which had not formed part of the original Army of the Indus but arrived later on rotational duty) and two companies of the 5th Native Infantry, together with two horse artillery guns, was sent from the cantonments towards the Lahore Gate to try and join up with Shelton from the Bala Hissar. For some reason the orders to Shelton to meet them in a pincer movement never arrived, and finding themselves being fired on from the city, the detachment was forced to retreat back to the cantonments. Communications between the city and the cantonments were becoming perilous with increasing number of Afghans occupying key positions on the land between the city and the cantonments, including Mahomed Shereef's fort and the walled Shah Bagh Gardens on the road towards the city. The walls of the fort and gardens were loopholed by the Afghans giving them critical vantage points over the road from the cantonments, and providing protective cover for accurate sniper fire. An order was sent to Nott in Kandahar to provide reinforcements, and Sale was ordered to return with his brigade from Gandamak. As a precaution, and a sign of the increasing seriousness of the situation, Macnaughten moved himself and his family from his residency in the Mission Compound on the edge of the cantonments to within its walls, and efforts were made to strengthen the defences.

4 November

The fort containing the commissariat, situated about half a mile from the cantonments, became under siege. It was defended by Lieutenant Warren, with around 100 sepoys, who sent a message to the cantonments for urgent reinforcements. Elphinstone's initial response was to send a company of the 37th Native Infantry with 11 camels carrying ammunition, but they could not get through the Afghan crossfire from Mahomed Shereef's fort and the high walls of the Shah Bagh Gardens. Two companies of HM 44th Foot were then sent to reinforce Warren but they too were defeated by Afghan gunfire and had to retire to the cantonments. In the evening yet a third attempt was made, this time with the intention of rescuing rather than reinforcing Warren with a party consisting largely of 5th Light Cavalry. They too could not withstand the accurate sniping from the fort and gardens, and with the loss of eight troopers and 14 seriously wounded retreated back inside the cantonments.

With only two days' worth of provisions in the cantonments, the implications of the potential loss of the commissariat fort became increasingly clear, and Elphinstone sent an order to Warren to hold out at all costs – though Warren later denied ever receiving the order. Elphinstone was urged

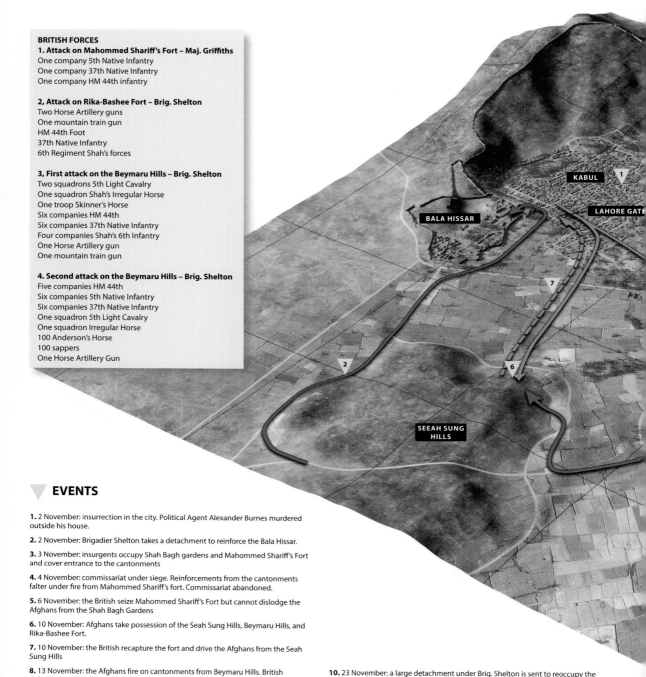

BRITISH FORCES
1. Attack on Mahommed Shariff's Fort – Maj. Griffiths
One company 5th Native Infantry
One company 37th Native Infantry
One company HM 44th infantry

2, Attack on Rika-Bashee Fort – Brig. Shelton
Two Horse Artillery guns
One mountain train gun
HM 44th Foot
37th Native Infantry
6th Regiment Shah's forces

3, First attack on the Beymaru Hills – Brig. Shelton
Two squadrons 5th Light Cavalry
One squadron Shah's Irregular Horse
One troop Skinner's Horse
Six companies HM 44th
Six companies 37th Native Infantry
Four companies Shah's 6th Infantry
One Horse Artillery gun
One mountain train gun

4. Second attack on the Beymaru Hills – Brig. Shelton
Five companies HM 44th
Six companies 5th Native Infantry
Six companies 37th Native Infantry
One squadron 5th Light Cavalry
One squadron Irregular Horse
100 Anderson's Horse
100 sappers
One Horse Artillery Gun

KABUL

BALA HISSAR

LAHORE GATE

SEEAH SUNG HILLS

▼ **EVENTS**

1. 2 November: insurrection in the city. Political Agent Alexander Burnes murdered outside his house.

2. 2 November: Brigadier Shelton takes a detachment to reinforce the Bala Hissar.

3. 3 November: insurgents occupy Shah Bagh gardens and Mahommed Shariff's Fort and cover entrance to the cantonments

4. 4 November: commissariat under siege. Reinforcements from the cantonments falter under fire from Mahommed Shariff's fort. Commissariat abandoned.

5. 6 November: the British seize Mahommed Shariff's Fort but cannot dislodge the Afghans from the Shah Bagh Gardens

6. 10 November: Afghans take possession of the Seah Sung Hills, Beymaru Hills, and Rika-Bashee Fort.

7. 10 November: the British recapture the fort and drive the Afghans from the Seah Sung Hills

8. 13 November: the Afghans fire on cantonments from Beymaru Hills. British dislodge them and they abandon their guns.

9. 22 November: Akbar Khan arrives in the city. The Afghans descend on Beymaru Village to cut off supplies to British. A British detachment fails to dislodge them from the village.

10. 23 November: a large detachment under Brig. Shelton is sent to reoccupy the Beymaru Hills and village. After fierce fighting the British have to abandon a gun and retreat to the cantonments

11. 22 December: Envoy Macnaughten murdered while negotiating the terms of retreat.

THE BRITISH RESPONSE TO THE KABUL INSURRECTION, 2–23 NOVEMBER 1841

The inadequate response of the British to initial disturbances in Kabul encouraged the growth of Afghan resistance over the next three weeks. Poor military leadership and the exposed siting of the cantonments and commissariat led to the British capitulation.

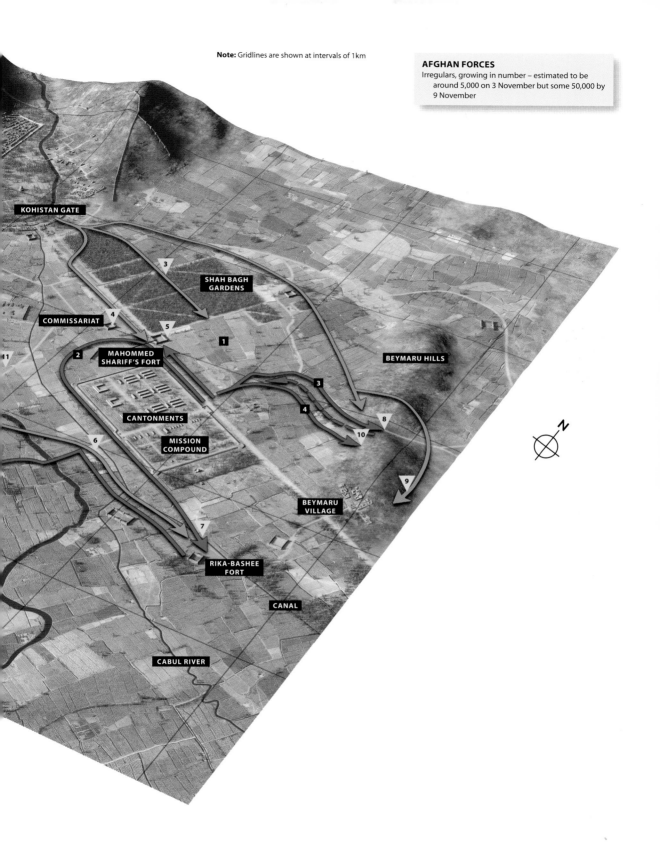

Note: Gridlines are shown at intervals of 1km

AFGHAN FORCES
Irregulars, growing in number – estimated to be
around 5,000 on 3 November but some 50,000 by
9 November

KOHISTAN GATE

3

SHAH BAGH
GARDENS

COMMISSARIAT

4

5

1

2

MAHOMMED
SHARIFF'S FORT

11

BEYMARU HILLS

3

CANTONMENTS

4

8

MISSION
COMPOUND

10

6

7

BEYMARU
VILLAGE

9

N

RIKA-BASHEE
FORT

CANAL

CABUL RIVER

ATTACK ON THE COMMISSARIAT, 4 NOVEMBER 1841 (PP. 62–63)

It was ill-advisedly decided that the British forces should be housed in cantonments (**1**), constructed some two miles from Kabul city, with poor defensive walls that were overlooked by the Beymaru Heights (**2**). An even worse decision was taken to place the commissariat containing all the provisions and medical supplies in an old fort half a mile away (**3**). The failure of the British to mount any effective response to the initial insurrection in the city on 2 November encouraged the Afghans to occupy the land between the city and the cantonments, including the walled Shah Bagh Gardens (**4**) and Mahomed Shereef's fort (**5**). On 4 November, the Afghans began to attack the commissariat, defended by Lieutenant Francis Warren (**6**) of the 5th Bengal Native Infantry together with some 100 sepoys (**7**). Warren, aged 39, who was described by a contemporary as 'a man of cool determined courage, who said little and always went about with a couple of bulldogs (**8**) at his heel', sent a message to the cantonments for urgent reinforcements. A company of the 37th Native Infantry, together with ammunition supplies, was dispatched but had to retreat because of the accurate sniping from the Shah Bagh Gardens and Mahomed Shereef's fort that overlooked the road from the cantonments. A second party of two companies from the 44th was sent but again were subjected to heavy fire, and with the loss of two Captains and three other officers wounded, had to withdraw (**9**). A further rescue attempt was made in the evening by a party of the 5th Light Cavalry but

with the loss of eight troopers and 14 seriously wounded, again they could not withstand the crossfire and had to retreat. Warren continued to send messages that the situation was now perilous, but was ordered by General Elphinstone to hold out at all costs, though Warren later denied receiving the order. Despite being urged by some of his officers to carry out a night attack, Elphinstone was reluctant to lose more men, and spent the whole night unable to make a decision. The Afghans were bringing ladders to storm the fort (**10**), and trying to mine one of the towers. Despite further urgent messages from Warren, Elphinstone decided to wait until morning. However, by then it was too late. Warren, faced with the annihilation of his men and no sign of reinforcements, had decided to evacuate the fort, escaping with the sepoys through a hole they had cut through one of the walls. On his arrival at the cantonments, and being called upon to state his reasons for abandoning the position, he offered to explain himself before a court of inquiry. No such inquiry was held, no doubt because it would have exposed Elphinstone's indecisiveness. The loss of the commissariat, leaving just two days' worth of supplies in the cantonments, was a major blow to the British, and encouraged more Afghans to join the rebellion. Just over two weeks later, the British were forced to negotiate a withdrawal of all their forces. Lieutenant Warren was killed during the retreat on 13 January, and there is a memorial to him at St Mary's Church in Nottingham.

by some of his officers to initiate a night attack on Mahomed Shereef's fort to dislodge the rebels, but he spent most of the night wrestling with the issue as he was reluctant to lose any more men. Despite further requests during the night from Warren, whose position was increasingly perilous with the Afghans bringing ladders to storm the fort, Elphinstone took the decision to wait until morning. However, by then it was too late to save the commissariat since Warren, with no sign of reinforcements despite his repeated requests, had abandoned his position and returned to the cantonments. He offered to defend himself in a court martial, but because Elphinstone's own indecision would then have been more openly exposed, no disciplinary action was taken against him.

6 November
The loss of the commissariat was a serious blow to the British and encouraged more Afghans, including the Qizilbashis, to join the growing rebellion. Large numbers of Afghan tribesmen were seen to be occupying hills towards the west of the cantonments, and at last there was a more robust response from the British when the decision was taken to storm Mahomed Shereef's fort. It took two hours to force a breach using three 9-pounder guns, and a storming party of three companies of infantrymen retook the fort, but it proved impossible to drive the Afghans from the Shah Bagh Gardens.

7 November
In Afghanistan there had long been a tradition of payments to tribal leaders in return for loyalty, and the British had continued the practice. Macnaughten sent messages via an intermediary to the tribal leaders of the Ghilzais and the Qizilbashis in the city, with the promise of large bribes should they help quell the insurrection. The offer of bribes continued over the next few days, and included the offer of rewards to kill the main leaders, but the chieftains, sensing the growing weakness of the British position, refused the overtures.

9 November
Brigadier Shelton was recalled from the Bala Hissar to provide further support for the cantonments. His presence was needed to provide some effective military leadership since Elphinstone had grown increasingly sick and depressed, and was unable to function properly as a commander. However, the abandonment of Shah Soojah in the Bala Hissar only provided further encouragement to the Afghans joining the uprising, and there were now estimated to be around 50,000 in and around the city. Shelton advocated an immediate retreat to Jalalabad but was overruled by Macnaughten.

10 November
With provisions running extremely low, the only realistic source of new supplies was the village of Beymaru towards the north of the cantonments. A large body of Afghan cavalry and foot soldiers took possession of the Seeah Sung hills and Beymaru Heights presumably with the intention of cutting off the British, and began occupying key forts dotted around, including the Rika-Bashee Fort opposite the cantonments, near the Kabul river. Brigadier Shelton was sent to capture the fort with a force consisting of two heavy artillery guns, one mountain gun, HM 44th Foot, the 37th Native Infantry, 6th Shah's Regiment, and Walker's Horse.

The Beymaru Heights, 1880. The Beymaru Heights provided an ideal position for Afghan forces to use to dominate the British cantonments below them. The cantonments in the photograph were built during the Second Afghan War, near the original site of those built by the British in 1840, but these more sensibly included the Beymaru Heights within the defence structures. (National Army Museum)

An advance storming party blew the gate but the hole was so narrow that only one or two soldiers could crawl in at a time, where, like lambs to the slaughter, they were mown down from within the fort. A small storming party of British and sepoy soldiers finally succeeded in entering the fort and the Afghan occupants, assuming they were the advance guard of a much larger force, abandoned their position. However, at that point a group of Afghan cavalry charged from the rear forcing the storming party to retreat further inside where nearly all were killed.

There was now fierce fighting between the Afghans and the main detachment of the 37th Native Infantry and the 44th, with the British faltering several times under Afghan cavalry charges. Shelton, for all his faults, showed considerable bravery in encouraging his men under exposed

Lieutenant Bird's heroic defence. During the attack on Rika-Bashee Fort on 10 November, the British advance guard found itself trapped inside the fort. The sole survivors were Lieutenant Bird and a sepoy who were down to five cartridges between them before being rescued by the main British contingent led by Colonel Shelton. (Anne S. K. Brown Military Collection, Brown University)

fire, and finally retook the fort. There they rescued the survivors of the storming party, a single British officer, Lt. Bird, and a sepoy, who had fought from behind a closed stable door for over 15 minutes, and who had just five cartridges left between them. Some 200 from the British force were killed or wounded. The Afghans then evacuated four other nearby forts, which were found to contain around 100 tons of grain. The British were able to remove half of this back to the cantonments before nightfall, but Shelton was reluctant to leave men there during the night, and by the next morning the remaining stores had been taken by the Afghans. However, the Rika-Bashee Fort remained in British hands. Its tower was blown to prevent it becoming reoccupied, and Shelton then moved towards the Seeah Sung Heights with heavy artillery guns. The Afghan cavalry retired from the hills, and the apparent success of the operations greatly heartened those watching from the cantonments.

13 November
A large body of Afghans began firing on the cantonments with 6-pounder and 4-pounder guns from the Beymaru Heights. At 3pm Shelton, with a strong force of 16 companies of infantrymen, and three squadrons and a troop of cavalry together with two horse artillery guns – one of which got stuck in the canals en route – was sent to dislodge the Afghans and recover their guns. There was heavy fighting with short-range, but inaccurate, firing from the British forces having little effect. However, the Afghans finally abandoned their guns, and the British spiked the 6-pounder and dragged the 4-pounder back to the cantonments.

14 November
General Nott in Kandahar received the orders to send reinforcements to Kabul and a brigade was dispatched but would take weeks to arrive. In the event, poor lines of communications through hostile territory, and worsening winter conditions forced the brigade to return to Kandahar on 8 December.

16 November
The success of the operations on the 13th lead to a lull in Afghan activity, although there were reports they were using the time to regroup and manufacture more ammunition in the city. The British considered whether it would make more military sense to abandon the cantonments and move to the well-fortified Bala Hissar, but the idea of the two-mile journey was rejected as being too hazardous, especially with so many sick and wounded. At this stage, the attacks from the Afghans, though aggressive, still appeared to be more opportunistic than part of a worked-out, coordinated strategy.

Brigadier Shelton. Colonel of the 44th Foot, Brigadier Shelton, was appointed second-in-command of the forces in Kabul on the arrival of his regiment on rotational duty in 1841. A cantankerous man, he openly despised his commander-in-chief, Elphinstone, and during the uprising would deliberately go to sleep during councils of war. (Essex Regimental Museum)

17 November

News came that any hope of relief from General Sale's brigade only 70 miles away was unfounded. Sale, though later criticized by some writers for his failure to return to Kabul, was in a difficult position, and initially may not have appreciated the very perilous situation facing the British forces in Kabul. Following discussions with his military command, he had concluded that returning would be too hazardous, and would have required abandoning over 300 sick and wounded to the mercy of the Ghilzais tribes. Instead, he moved his brigade to Jalalabad as a defensive base, to await reinforcements from Peshawar through the Khyber Pass. This also turned out to be a false hope since a relief force under Brigadier Wild had been unable to force the pass. Macnaughten wrote to Sale imploring him to return from Jalalabad: 'Our situation is a desperate one if you do not immediately return, and I beg you will do so without a moment's delay. We have now been besieged for fourteen days and without your assistance are utterly unable to carry on any offensive action.' The letter reveals that Macnaughten finally appreciated the very real military dilemma for the British in the cantonments in that they simply had insufficient forces to carry out both offensive and defensive actions at the same time.

18 November

Macnaughten reconsidered the options open to the British. Once again, moving to the Bala Hissar was rejected, and any retreat to Jalalabad was equally hazardous and would be seen as a sign of defeat. Soldiers were now on half rations, but if more supplies could be bought from the village of Beymaru, Macnaughten estimated they could stay in the cantonments for another eight days in the hope that relief from Nott might appear, or that the situation would somehow change in the meantime.

22 November

There were reports that Akbar Khan had entered the city, and taken more strategic control, appreciating that the most effective apporach was to avoid direct attacks and simply starve the British into submission. Cutting off any further supplies from the village of Beymaru would be critical to this strategy, and large bodies of Afghan cavalrymen were seen to ascend the hills overlooking the village, while Akbar Khan sent emissaries to persuade the villagers to stop selling any supplies to the British. A British detachment with a wing of the 37th Native Infantry, two squadrons of Irregular Horse, one squadron Light Cavalry, and a mountain train gun was sent to forestall the Afghans taking the village but found it already occupied by a small number of Afghans. For six hours the British detachment fired their gun ineffectively on Beymaru, but found themselves far more susceptible to accurate shooting from Afghan snipers.

23 November

It was clear that the reoccupation of Beymaru village would be vital to the survival of the British, and Shelton was ordered to occupy the Beymaru Heights and capture the village with a large force – almost half the garrison – consisting of five companies of HM 44th Foot, six companies of the 5th Native Infantry, six companies of the 37th Native Infantry, a squadron of 5th Cavalry, a squadron of irregular horse, 100 Anderson's Horse, one horse artillery gun, and 100 sappers. Shelton had recommended that the best tactic was to take the hills and village at the same time but he was overruled. Moving silently at night, with great difficulty they dragged a single gun up on the hill and began firing on the village, causing a large number of Afghans to leave. A storming party was sent, but once again accurate fire from the Afghans remaining in the village, estimated to be fewer than 50, made it difficult to secure the village. With daybreak, large numbers of Afghan reinforcements were seen to be coming from the city to occupy hills and reinforce the village.

The Afghans began firing from a hill opposite the British, and were amassing forces in a gorge separating the two hills that formed the Beymaru Heights. Shelton left five companies on the edge of the hill overlooking the village, and took the remainder of his force to the top of the hill. The British then made an error in forming two defensive squares of infantry with the cavalry drawn up at the rear. This tactic might have been effective in a conventional cavalry attack (Shelton was a veteran of Waterloo), but the Afghans sensibly avoided any direct charge, and largely resorted to accurate long-distance sniping with *jezails* from the protection of cover. The single British gun had made a serious impact on the Afghans, but its vent became overheated, making it unsafe for the gunners. Taking just one gun for such an exercise was against all military practice for that very reason, but Shelton had taken the risk on being informed that the second mountain gun was still being repaired, and would not be ready until the next day. More Afghans had moved from the Shah Bagh Gardens to the plain between the hill and the cantonments in order to cut off any further reinforcements, suggesting that a rather more sophisticated strategy than had been the case in the early days of the insurrection was now in play.

The Afghans felt sufficiently powerful to make a successful rush for the gun from the concealed gulley. Many on the British side had lost heart, with the cavalry refusing orders to charge, and one of the squares collapsing. There was a brief period of recovery by the British who recaptured the gun, but despite repeated requests no extra gun or reinforcements were sent from the cantonments. The Afghans continued to rain accurate sniper fire on the remaining square with the front men and artillery 'literally mown down' according to one observer, and sensing the British force had lost heart, they made a sudden concerted charge, breaking the square, recapturing the gun, and forcing the British to retreat back to the cantonments.

THE RETREAT, 1842

NEGOTIATIONS FOR WITHDRAWAL

The rout on the Beymaru Heights was greeted with dismay in the cantonments, and, as Shelton wryly noted, 'concluded all exterior operations'. The British were now so weakened and demoralized that the Afghans could have probably secured the cantonments, but they failed to do so, suggesting there was no intention at this stage to destroy the British forces, but rather to see them leave the country.

Once again, the option of moving forces to the fortified citadel of the Bala Hissar was considered but again rejected as too hazardous an operation. Despite their physical proximity within the cantonments, Macnaughten and Elphinstone were largely communicating with each other by letter, and on 24 November Elphinstone wrote to Macnaughten saying he felt it was 'no longer feasible to maintain our position in this country'. The shortage of supplies and lack of prospect of any relief convinced Macnaughten that the time had come to negotiate.

The initial discussion with Afghan chiefs was unpromising with demands from the tribal leader Sultan Mohammad for a complete capitulation and surrender of all arms, and the abandonment of Shah Soojah. Macnaughten dismissed the demands preferring to play for more time in the hope of reinforcements. Shah Soojah's own position was increasingly perilous. Earlier in the rebellion a number of the leaders who favoured the Sadozai royalty had tried to persuade him to join in a nationalist uprising against the British, but he refused to abandon his backers. He now remained holed up in the Bala Hissar, incredulous that despite repeated requests no substantial reinforcements were sent from the cantonments.

It was clear that no reinforcements would come from Kandahar or elsewhere, and starvation was setting in. On 8 December Elphinstone informed Macnaughten there were just three days' rations left for troops, with no forage for horses or cattle, and over 600 sick and wounded in hospital. Supported by his senior command, he urged immediate negotiations, and three days later, Macnaughten met with the Afghan tribal chiefs with a proposed treaty. The draft terms accepted that the great majority of Afghans did not support Shah Soojah. The British troops would leave Kabul unmolested and 'with all practicable expedition', accompanied by tribal chiefs, with provisions to be supplied to the British on payment. Other garrisons in Kabul would similarly be abandoned. Shah Soojah would be permitted either to remain in Kabul or to accompany the British, and once the troops had arrived in India, Dost Mohammad and his family would return to Kabul. If Shah Soojah chose to remain in the city he would then be allowed safe passage to India. Four British officers would remain as hostages to guarantee the terms. Notwithstanding the retirement of the British troops from Afghanistan, the draft treaty noted, 'there will always be friendship between that nation and the English'.

The terms were agreed with the provision that the British should leave within three days. Only Akbar Khan disagreed, arguing the British should leave the next day and there should be no requirements to provide them with provisions. However, though a forceful leader, he was not in command of the rebels – before he had arrived in the city, his cousin Mohammed Zaman Khan Barakzai had been selected as leader under the title of Amir of the Faithful, with two of the leaders of the uprising as his *wazir* and military commander-in-chief.

Under the treaty the troops should have started evacuating on 15 December. The remaining British troops within the Bala Hissar had left two days earlier, but there were continuing delays with heavy snowfalls, increasing demands from the Afghans for the handing over of more guns and hostages, and the failure to supply the British with adequate provisions as agreed under the treaty. A new date for the departure, 22 December, was fixed.

Macnaughten sensed that he might still recover the situation by playing on the disunity between the Afghan tribal leaders, and attempted to offer large sums to the Ghilzais to side with Shah Soojah. A number of Durrani leaders, uncomfortable with the agreement that Shah Soojah would be required to abandon his throne, were secretly encouraged by Macnaughten to approach Shah Soojah to suggest he remain on the throne with the Barakzais resuming their traditional role as *wazir*. Soojah rejected the proposition, but Akbar Khan, intent on increasing his own authority, decided to expose the continuing untrustworthiness of the British by sending a private message to Macnaughten. This contained proposals that Akbar would persuade the Ghilzais to join British troops in recapturing Mahmood Khan's fort, the British could delay their departure until the spring, Shah Soojah would remain as king with Akbar Khan to be appointed *wazir*, and Akbar would be paid an annuity by the British.

Against advice that this was merely a dangerous ruse, Macnaughten agreed to meet Akbar Khan on 23 December on the banks of the river about 600 yards from the cantonments. He was accompanied

Shah Soojah was left abandoned by the British forces in the Bala Hissar. For some months after the British retreated from Kabul he was able to stay in control supported by a number of tribal leaders who were still loyal to the Sadozai royal family. However, in April 1842 he was assassinated by the son of a rival leader. (© Peter & Renate Nahum)

by just three officers and a few cavalry, while Akbar Khan was accompanied by a number of tribal chiefs, and, as Macnaughten remarked at the time, rather more armed men than seemed necessary for what was supposed to be a secret conference. Akbar asked Macnaughten if he wished to proceed along the lines of the secret proposals he had sent. Macnaughten agreed, and the duplicity was exposed. Macnaughten was then seized and murdered, and by all accounts Akbar Khan fired the first shots with a pistol that Macnaughten had presented to him only a few days earlier. One of the other British officers was killed, but two managed to escape back to safety.

Back in the cantonments the British took no action with Elphinstone claiming he had not realized Macnaughten had been killed and had assumed he had gone with Akbar to the city, while others argued they had clearly seen what had happened from the walls of the cantonments. The Afghan leaders sent proposals to continue negotiations on the original treaty for the evacuation and Major Pottinger, now the senior political officer following the deaths of Burnes and Macnaughten, was appointed to lead negotiations. Pottinger still argued the case for moving the troops to the Bala Hisser but was overruled. Akbar Khan was clearly now in a dominant position, and eventually on 1 January a new treaty was signed by 18 Afghan leaders, including Akbar Khan. There would now be six British hostages to be returned once Dost Mohammad and other Afghan detainees reached Peshawar. All guns except for six horse artillery guns and three mule guns, would be handed over to the Afghans. Jalalabad, Ghazni, and Kandahar would be similarly evacuated. Two Afghan leaders would accompany the British force from Kabul and there would be no molestation along the route. The British would leave 'and shall not return', but 'friendship and goodwill' would continue to exist between the British and Afghan governments, with the Afghan Government committed to making future treaties only with the British. No mention was made of the position of Shah Soojah.

Death of Macnaughten. Less than two months after the initial insurrection in Kabul, Macnaughten was trying to negotiate an honourable withdrawal from Afghanistan. In a desperate move he was prepared to bribe Akbar Khan to support the British. During a secret meeting just outside the cantonments, his double-dealings were exposed and he was murdered by Akbar Khan. (Author's collection)

6 January

Preparations were made to evacuate the cantonments, although winter weather conditions were grim. A tribal chief meant to accompany the British did not appear, but sent a message stating that he would not be ready for at least 24 hours. Pottinger advised waiting but was overruled. A breach was cut through the walls of the cantonments and at 9.30am an advance guard set off in deep snow under the command of Brigadier Anquetil. It consisted of HM 44th Foot, 4th Irregular Horse, Skinner's Horse, two horse artillery guns, and sappers, together with wives and children. At the time there was no direct route along the river to Jalalabad because of steep gorges (it now contains the main A01 highway between Kabul and Jalalabad, and is considered to be one of the most dangerous roads in the world) and the mountain route through the passes was chosen. They had rations for just five and half days.

Speed was of the essence and the whole force – some 700 European soldiers, 3,800 sepoys, and around 12,000 camp followers – should have left by noon. Elphinstone's intention was to reach Khord Kabul on the first day and Tezin, some 30 miles away, on the second, but everything took much longer than planned. A temporary bridge of gun waggons was meant to have been constructed over the Kabul River, but it was not ready until midday. By then the orderly march of the advance guard across the river was made impossible because of the enormous number of camp followers, leading to chaotic scenes at the river crossing. The main body of troops under Shelton, consisting of the 5th and 37th Native Infantry, Anderson's Horse, Shah's 6th Regiment, and two horse artillery guns began leaving during the day. A rearguard of the 54th Native Infantry, 5th Cavalry, and two 6-pounder horse artillery guns was left to man the walls of the cantonments, watching Afghans moving in to plunder what they could find. They were only able to leave by early evening, the guns were abandoned, and some 50 men were lost to opportunistic attacks.

The army encamped overnight at Begramu, about five miles from Kabul, with the rearguard not arriving until 2am. There were no tents, and conditions were freezing, with little in the way of food or fires. A number of British and camp followers died of the cold, and many in the Shah's forces simply deserted, presumably to join their fellow countrymen in Kabul.

7 January

At 7.30am the advance guard set off, but found its route encumbered by abandoned baggage and camp followers who had decided to leave earlier. The intention had been to reach Khord Kabul, but after five miles the order was given to halt at Bhoodarak. By now most of the baggage had been abandoned, and all but two of the guns had been spiked because the horses were too weak to pull them. Those in the rear and on the flanks were being attacked by Afghans, and a large body of Afghan cavalry charged the column carrying away camels and baggage.

8 January

There was disorder in the camp and many had frozen to death during the night. The Afghans were increasing in numbers. A section of the 44th, together with some cavalry, drove them back, and took command of the heights. Akbar Khan was in the vicinity, and he agreed to protect the troops on payment of 15,000 rupees and the handing over of more hostages (Pottinger, Lawrence and Mackenzie) to guarantee the evacuation from Jalalabad.

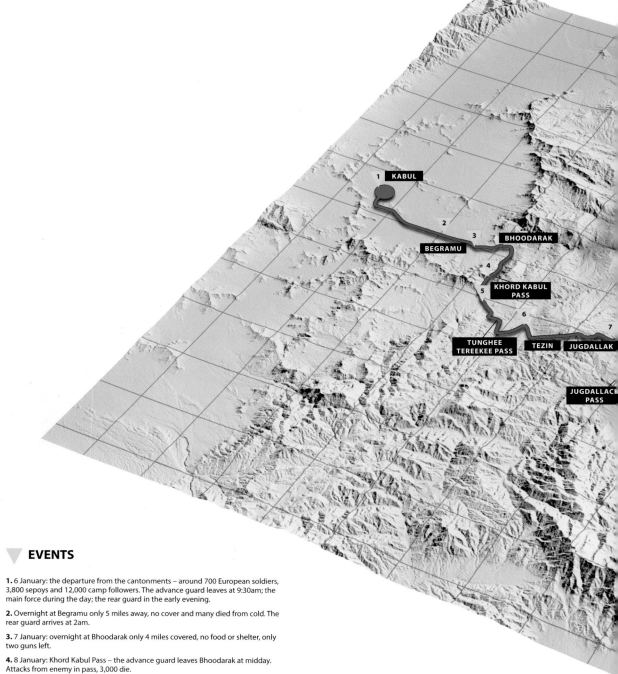

Map labels:
- KABUL (1)
- 2
- BEGRAMU
- 3
- BHOODARAK
- 4
- 5
- KHORD KABUL PASS
- 6
- 7
- TUNGHEE TEREEKEE PASS
- TEZIN
- JUGDALLAK
- JUGDALLACK PASS

▼ EVENTS

1. 6 January: the departure from the cantonments – around 700 European soldiers, 3,800 sepoys and 12,000 camp followers. The advance guard leaves at 9:30am; the main force during the day; the rear guard in the early evening.

2. Overnight at Begramu only 5 miles away, no cover and many died from cold. The rear guard arrives at 2am.

3. 7 January: overnight at Bhoodarak only 4 miles covered, no food or shelter, only two guns left.

4. 8 January: Khord Kabul Pass – the advance guard leaves Bhoodarak at midday. Attacks from enemy in pass, 3,000 die.

5. 9 January: wives and children taken prisoner.

6. 10 January: night march to Tezin. Ambush in the Tunghee Tereekee Pass, 4,000 survive – fighting force consist of 50 horse-artillerymen, 250 infantry and150 cavalry troopers.

7. 11 January: Jugdallack. Advance guard arrives at 3pm under continual fire. Negotiations with Akbar Khan, Elphinstone and Shelton taken prisoner.

8. 12 January: Jugdallack Pass. The remaining force leaves at 8pm. The pass is blocked by holly. Heavy attacks. Less than 200 get through.

9. 13 January: Gandamack. Last stand of the 44th.

10. 13 January: Last six cavalry seek refuge in Futtehabad. Two killed in the village, the remaining four killed riding to Jalalabad.

11. 13 January: Dr Brydon reaches Jalalabad.

THE RETREAT FROM KABUL, 1842

The British force in Kabul, some 4,000 soldiers and 12,000 camp-followers, negotiated a retreat in mid-winter to Jalalabad less than 90 miles away. Five days later, few had survived the cold, lack of supplies and continual attacks from Afghan tribesmen.

Note: Gridlines are shown at intervals of 10km

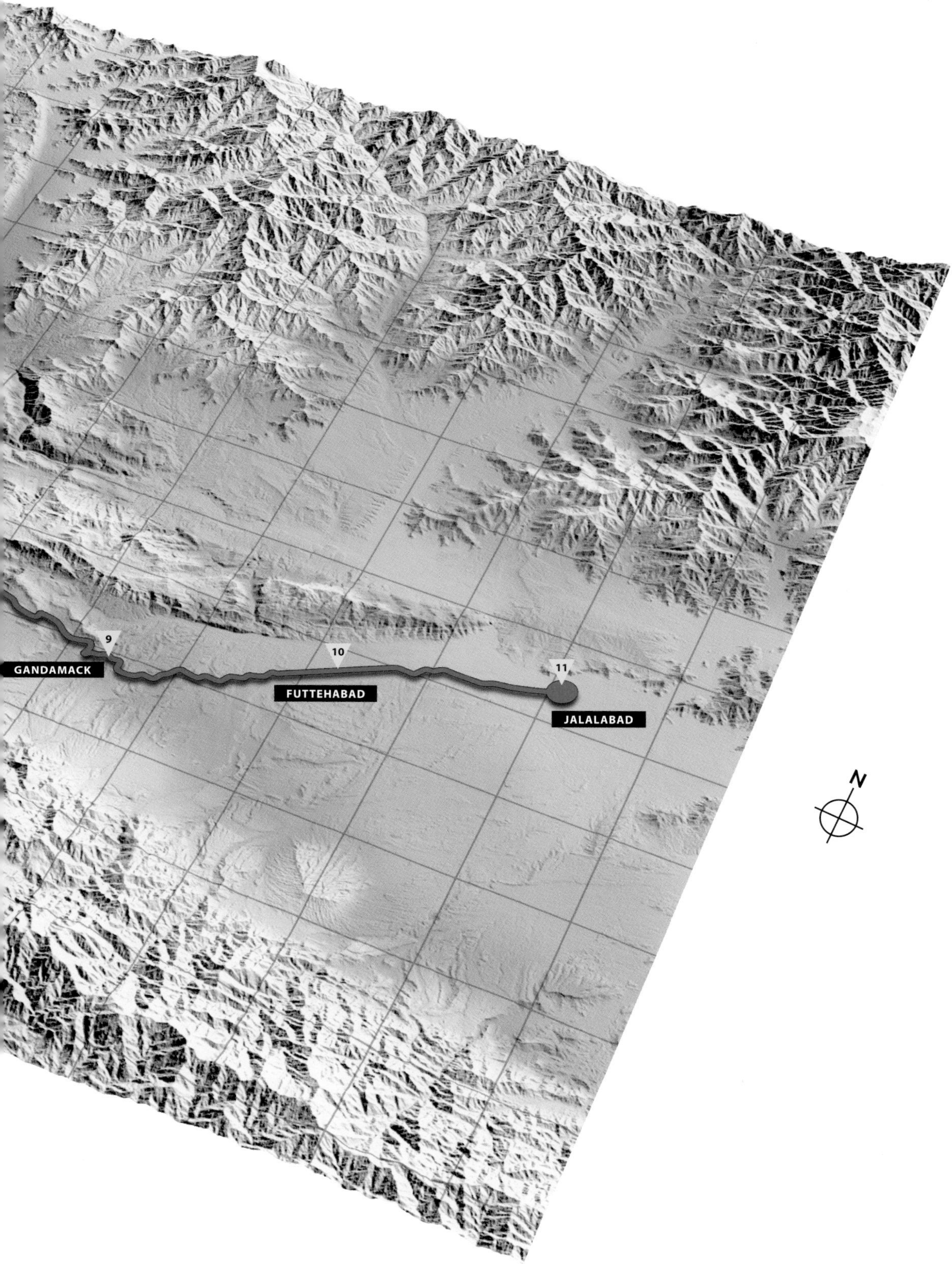

9
GANDAMACK
10
FUTTEHABAD
11
JALALABAD
N

Last Stand at Gandamak. The remnants of the 44th, who had survived the horrors of Jagdalak Pass, were surrounded at Gandamak, only a few miles from Jalalabad. Refusing to surrender, they fought a last stand, and all but a few were killed. Captain Souter had wrapped the regimental standard round his waist, and was taken hostage because he was assumed to be someone of importance. (Essex Regimental Museum)

THE RETREAT OF THE BRITISH FORCE FROM KABUL

The confusion was such that the advance guard did not set off until midday with the 5th Native Infantry in front, and once again the presence of camp followers, desperate to escape, only caused more chaos. The Afghans continued to launch attacks on the rear column seizing plunder, and a number of European children and wives were carried off. Entering the Khord Kabul Pass, the force found itself under sustained attack from the rear, protected by the 44th and the 37th Native Infantry. The crush within the pass was so great that at times the rearguard had to remain stationary, which resulted in it sustaining heavy losses under fire.

9 January
Again there were no proper orders to leave, and in the confusion troops began to move off at random. Akbar Khan then sent messages that he was not yet ready to provide sufficient protection, and everyone was told to halt for the day. Akbar proposed that married men and their families be put under his protection, and a group including wives and children was taken to the Khord Kabul forts about two miles away. They were to remain captives for over nine months.

10 January
In the usual confusion, the remaining soldiers and camp followers began the ascent from Khord Kabul through the narrow pass at Tunghee Tarekee towards Tezin around 15 miles away. At Tunghee Tarekee, the rearguard suffered a heavy attack from Ghilzai tribesmen, who would first shoot from behind cover and then charge. The British forces were down to about 70 of the 44th, 50 of the 5th Cavalry, and one 6-pounder gun. By now nearly 12,000 of those who had left Kabul had died, leaving around 4,000. Akbar Khan offered to escort the remnants to Jalalabad if they would disarm, but Elphinstone refused. Seeing little prospect of provisions at Tezin, Elphinstone decided the only hope of survival was to march at night and be through the Jagdalak Pass by early morning in the hope there would be insufficient time for the Afghans to mass a large enough force to cut them off.

11 January

Progress remained painfully slow, and in the morning the force was still some ten miles from the entrance to the Jagdalak Pass. It took the advance guard, now under almost continual fire from Afghans in the surrounding hills, until 3pm to reach Jagdalak. By the time the rest of the exhausted force arrived, they found themselves pinned down by deadly sniper fire from *jezails* and unable to move. In the late afternoon a message arrived from Akbar Khan suggesting a conference with Elphinstone, and clutching at straws that he might save the remaining force, Elphinstone, Shelton, and another officer departed to Akbar's camp for the meeting.

12 January

Elphinstone and his officers were treated courteously, but spent all day achieving very little. Akbar Khan was accompanied by the local Ghilzai chiefs who were in control of the pass, and he seemed to be genuinely trying to persuade them to give safe conduct to the British in return for payments of large sums of money. Meanwhile, Brigadier Anquetil, left in command of the remaining force, had given up hope of seeing Elphinstone and the officers return. He was correct in his assumption for by the evening they had indeed been taken hostage to join the existing prisoners, and Anquetil decided the only option was to proceed, leaving the sick and wounded behind.

Whether Akbar's negotiations were genuine or simply a ploy to delay the march is difficult to tell. However, by the time the British reached the entrance to the pass it had been blocked with a barrier of thick holly oak, with Afghans on all sides firing down and making occasional charges. In scenes of terrible brutality and confusion, with soldiers forced to tear gaps through the holly with their bare hands, the pass became a killing ground.

Lady Sale. Married to Colonel Sale, the formidable Lady Sale was one of those taken hostage on 9 January, surviving almost nine months in captivity. Her diary, full of sharp insights, became a best seller in London where she was feted as the 'Grenadier in Petticoats'. On her gravestone in Cape Town are the words, 'Underneath this stone reposes all that could die of Lady Sale'. (© Peter & Renate Nahum)

Entering the Khord Kabul Pass. This photograph was taken by the American anthropologist and Afghan historian Louis Dupree on 8 January 1963, during his walk of the retreat, but the entrance to the Khord Kabul Pass would have been unchanged from the time when the British forces found themselves crushed and under sustained attack from the rear. (Photo by Louis Dupree, permission of Nancy Hatch Dupree on behalf of the Afghanistan Centre at Kabul University)

JAGDALAK PASS, 12 JANUARY 1842 (PP. 78–79)

The British force, consisting of around 700 British soldiers, 3,800 sepoys, and 12,000 camp followers had left Kabul on 6 January to retreat to Jalalabad, some 90 miles away. Five days later they reached Jagdalak. By then the wintery conditions and continuous attacks from Afghan tribesmen had caused terrible losses, with British forces now amounting to just 70 of HM 44th Foot, 50 of the 5th Light Cavalry, and around 4,000 camp followers. Women and children and some officers had already been taken hostage. In the afternoon of 11 January, Akbar Khan, son of Dost Mohammad whom the British had deposed, proposed a conference with the British commanders in order to try and secure an agreement with local tribesmen and safe conduct through the passes. General Elphinstone, Brigadier Shelton, and Captain Johnson departed for the meeting leaving Brigadier Anquetil in command of the remaining forces. Most of the next day was spent in fruitless discussions with tribal leaders and Akbar Khan , while the British forces languished at Jagdalak, with very little shelter and being continuously fired upon by the Afghans embedded in the hills. By the evening Elphinstone, suspecting treachery, by some accounts sent a note to Brigadier Anquetil telling him to push on. In any event, Anquetil had given up hope of seeing the officers return – and they were indeed taken hostage to join the other British prisoners. It is unclear whether Akbar Khan was genuine in his efforts to restrain the local tribesmen, or had been playing for time to allow an even greater build-up of forces whose aim was to destroy the army. The remaining British set off about an hour after dark, but by the time they reached Jagdalak Pass, they were being fired on from all sides by Afghan snipers embedded in the hills (**1**). The pass was some two miles long with a narrow defile surrounded by precipitous heights (**2**). At the summit, two barriers of about 6ft high prickly holly oak branches had been placed to block the whole defile (3), and according to Dr Brydon, 'the only European to reach Jalalabad, 'The confusion now was terrible; all discipline was at an end.' The Afghans rushed in causing terrible casualties (**4**), with 12 officers, including Brigadier Anquetil, being killed. Infantry officers and men struggled with their bare hands to clear the holly barrier (**5**) but once an opening had been made cavalrymen rode over them through the gap (**6**). Some accounts suggest that in their fury the infantry fired on their own cavalry. According to a sepoy, Subedar Sita Ram, who was wounded and taken prisoner by the Afghans, 'We were attacked in front, in the rear, and from the tops of hills. In truth it was hell itself.' Of the British forces, just 20 officers and 45 soldiers of the 44th, and around a dozen cavalry managed to survive the pass. Most of the campfollowers had been killed or succumbed to the cold, though a few straggled through later.

Taken during the Second Afghan War (1878–80), this photo of Gandamak shows the rocky hill near the village of Gandamak on which the survivors of the 44th fought their last stand some 40 years earlier. (Essex Regimental Museum)

13 January

Of the remaining British forces, only some 20 officers, 45 infantry, and around a dozen cavalry managed to get through Jagdalak Pass. The officers and infantry reached the village of Gandamak, where they felt obliged to leave the road to take up a defensive position on a small hill just outside the village. They had only 20 muskets and two rounds of ammunition left. They were rapidly surrounded by Afghans who initially approached without firing and tried to persuade them to hand over their weapons. However, they were rebuffed, and the Afghans once again used long-distance fire from *jezails* to cut the survivors down before charging. Nearly all of the remnants of the 44th were killed, including 18 officers, though a few were taken prisoner.

The dozen cavalrymen had tried to ride on to Jalalabad but six were soon killed, with the remainder reaching the village of Futtehabad, only 16 miles from their goal. Initially welcomed by villagers, they were then attacked and two were killed. The remaining four managed to escape, but three were killed just four miles from Jalalabad leaving Dr Brydon on a wounded pony as the sole European to have survived the whole route from Kabul.

LEFT
Captain Talbot. Aged only 19, Captain Talbot served under Sir Robert Sale during the defence of the siege of Jalalabad. He was the officer on duty on 13 January 1842 who first spotted Dr Brydon through his telescope. He later became Chief Commissioner of the Dublin Metropolitan Police and died in 1914. (Image courtesy of the Somerset Military Museum Trust)

FAR LEFT
Dr Brydon. There were other survivors of the retreat from Kabul – officers and families taken hostage, and many sepoys who eventually made their way back to Kabul – but Dr Brydon was the only European who managed to reach Jalalabad. He died in Scotland in 1873, aged 61. (National Army Museum)

AFTERMATH

THE POSITION IN AFGHANISTAN

In Kabul, Shah Soojah had remained in the Bala Hissar with some 2,000 of his own troops, initially hoping that he would still be rescued by the British. When it became obvious that this would not be the case he played on the ever-present divisions within the Afghan tribal leadership inside the city to continue as national leader. He was able to secure a temporary agreement that would allow him to remain as king, with Zaman Khan (Akbar Khan's cousin who was jealous of Akbar's growing power) becoming *wazir* and Amanaullah Khan as viceroy. However, internal jealousies and tensions, especially over the payment and control of Afghan forces, destabilized the situation, and in April 1842 Shah Soojah was assassinated by a Barakzai. Shah Soojah's son was installed as king, but the city was now effectively in a state of anarchy.

Kandahar had remained in control of a large force of 6,000 troops commanded by General Nott, and was successfully resisting attacks from Durrani tribesmen. However, the city was almost lost in March when Nott led most of his force, including all the cavalry, to attack a large body of Afghans amassing in nearby hills. The enemy refused to engage, and they appear to have been a lure to persuade Nott to leave the city. Leaving a force of cavalry to delay Nott, the main body of Afghans doubled backed to attack the city walls at night, and might have succeeded in taking the city had it not been for fierce resistance from the remaining British infantry defending the city. If Kandahar had fallen, it is doubtful that Nott could have recaptured it without sustaining an immense number of causalities, but as it was, he was able to re-enter the city on 12 March. The failure of the attack caused Afghan resistance in the region to collapse.

Meanwhile, the city of Jalalabad, containing Brigadier Sale's brigade (the 13th Foot, 35th Bengal Native Infantry, a squadron of 5th Bengal Light Cavalry, a troop of loyal Afghan irregular horse, and gunners

Jalalabad. Following the destruction of the British forces on the retreat from Kabul, Colonel Sale and his brigade found themselves besieged in Jalalabad by a large body of Afghan forces led by Akbar Khan. (© Peter & Renate Nahum)

Sortie from Jalalabad. Supplies were running short during the siege of Jalalabad. On 1 April 1842 around 200 men of the HM 13th Regiment and 200 of the 35th Native Infantry managed to capture some 500 sheep and goats from the Afghans. Many of the men were in shirtsleeves because of the hot weather. (Image courtesy of the Somerset Military Museum Trust)

and sappers) was under lengthy siege from Akbar Khan, and various indecisive skirmishes had taken place between November and April. At the end of January, troops managed to replenish supplies by capturing nearly 200 bullocks and around 750 sheep – a similar sortie at the beginning of April secured another 500 sheep and goats. A major earthquake had severely damaged the walls of the garrison in February, but the Afghans failed to take advantage of the situation, and the walls were quickly repaired. On 13 February, Sale received intelligence that General Pollock had arrived at Peshawar, but because of delays in preparing the army, Pollock asked Sale to hold out at least until the end of March. Sale's forces amounted to 2,263 fit for duty, and some 195 unfit, with full rations for British soldiers for 70 days, and native soldiers on half rations. By the beginning of April there were conflicting rumours as to whether Pollock's force had secured the Khyber Pass, while at the same time there were reports that Akbar Khan was to return to Kabul to deal with insurrections in the city. Sale held a council of war, and with ammunition running out, decided that the time was ripe for a decisive attack on the Afghan forces. On 7 April Sale ordered an aggressive and successful attack on Akbar Khan's forces, some 6,000 men positioned about three miles from the city, and forced him to retreat back to Kabul. British losses were 14 killed and 66 wounded. Two days later, news came that Pollock's Army of Retribution had successfully forced the Khyber Pass.

THE ARMY OF RETRIBUTION

The new Tory Government under Peel was intent on abandoning any further involvement in Afghanistan. Lord Ellenborough, Auckland's successor as Governor General, arrived in February 1843, and was determined that there should be one last show of strength to ensure departure from the country with honour. A force of around 6,000, known as the Army of Retribution, was to be commanded by General Pollock, who had learnt much about the challenges of mountainous guerrilla warfare in the Nepalese wars some 35 years earlier. He spent several months undertaking careful logistical planning in Peshawar, building up his force and its resources, before finally setting

Army of Retribution, 1842

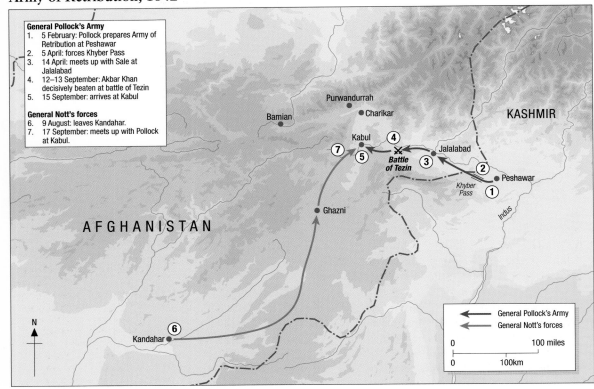

General Pollock's Army
1. 5 February: Pollock prepares Army of Retribution at Peshawar
2. 5 April: forces Khyber Pass
3. 14 April: meets up with Sale at Jalalabad
4. 12–13 September: Akbar Khan decisively beaten at battle of Tezin
5. 15 September: arrives at Kabul

General Nott's forces
6. 9 August: leaves Kandahar.
7. 17 September: meets up with Pollock at Kabul.

out in early April. A previous attempt to storm the Kyber Pass in January had failed, so Pollock employed the tactic of crowning the heights at the entrance to the pass with infantry, including a number using the long-range Afghan *jezails*, to bring down fire on the enemy from the rear. On entering the Khyber Pass the order of march was:

Advance Guard (Brigadier Wild)
One company 9th Queen's Regiment
One company 26th Native Infantry
Three companies 30th Regiment Native Infantry
Two companies 33rd Regiment Native Infantry
Nine pieces of artillery and sappers and miners
Two squadrons 3rd Dragoons
One squadron 1st Native Cavalry
Two companies 53rd Regiment Native Infantry
One squadron 1st Cavalry

Rearguard (General M'Caskill)
Three artillery guns
10th Light Cavalry
Two squadrons Irregular Cavalry
Two squadrons 3rd Dragoons
Two horse artillery guns
Three companies 60th Regiment Native Infantry
One company 6th Regiment Native Infantry
One company HM 9th Regiment of Foot

Infantry columns for crowning heights
Right crowning column
Two companies HM 9th Regiment of Foot
Four companies 26th Regiment Native Infantry with 400 *jezailchis*
Seven companies 30th Regiment

Native Infantry
Three companies 60th Regiment Native Infantry
Four companies 64th Regiment Native Infantry
One company and a half HM 9th Regiment of Foot

Left crowning column
Two companies HM 9th Regiment of Foot

Four companies 26th Regiment Native Infantry with 200 *jezailchis*
Seven companies 53rd Regiment Native Infantry
Three companies 60th Regiment Native Infantry
Four and a half companies 64th Regiment Native Infantry
One company and a half HM 9th Regiment of Foot

MARCH ON TO KABUL

There was resistance at the entrance to the pass, which had been blocked, but Pollock's tactic of sending columns in advance to secure the heights, and outflanking the Afghans paid off. Extracts from Pollock's orders at the time provide a flavour of his military thoroughness and skills:

> The officers entrusted with the command of the parties which are to flank the rear-guard on the heights must give the most vigilant attention to the important duty of preventing men from hurrying in advance of it; its rear must never be left exposed to fire from the heights.
>
> The force to be under arms tomorrow morning at half-past three o'clock, ready to move forward... No fires are to be lighted on any account; no drums to beat, or bugles to be sounded.
>
> The whole of the cavalry will be so placed by Brigadier White that any attempt at an attack from the low hills on the right may be frustrated.

Pollock reached Jalalabad on 14 April, meeting up with Sale's force. There then followed a lengthy period when Lord Ellenborough, who had long opposed the whole Afghan invasion, appeared to send conflicting orders as to whether or not Pollock should advance on to Kabul. News of the loss of Elphinstone's force had reached London in March, and that month Ellenborough had urged Pollock to deal the Afghan's 'a heavy and decisive blow'. However, a month later he was stating that the main goal was to secure the release of the prisoners still held by Akbar Khan, and then to ensure the security of the forces by withdrawing speedily back to India. Pollock was convinced that a withdrawal at this point would be seen as defeat. Nott had been told by Ellenborough to leave Kandahar but Pollock send a countermand

Lord Ellenborough. A Tory politician who succeeded Lord Auckland as Governor General in 1842, Lord Ellenborough was determined that the British should cease meddling in Afghan affairs. However, following the destruction of the British force from Kabul, he authorized the Army of Retribution to inflict a decisive blow against the Afghans in order to restore British pride. (Author's collection)

Sniping with accurate *jezails* from defensive positions was a highly effective Afghan tactic used in the mountainous passes of Afghanistan. This painting, though from the initial invasion, illustrates clearly the crowning tactics extensively used by General Pollock's Army of Retribution. The top left-hand corner shows British soldiers about to dislodge Afghan snipers. (Author's collection)

ordering him to stay. Over the next two months, Ellenborough and Pollock appeared to work at cross purposes, with Pollock deliberately obfuscating and demonstrating his characteristic obstinacy in relation to orders he felt were unjustified. Finally, in July Ellenborough sent instructions that both Pollock and Nott should retire to India, but could do so by advancing on Kabul if they considered their forces sufficient. Carefully leaving the critical decisions to the commanders on the spot, he stressed that the loss of another army would be 'fatal to our government in India', but equally that he did not undervalue the aid the successful march to Kabul would bring to the British Government.

Pollock received news from Nott that he was prepared to withdraw from Kandahar via Kabul. He then left Jalalabad on 20 August, also destined for Kabul, with a force of around 8,000 consisting of Sale's brigade, the 3rd Dragoons, the 1st Native Cavalry, a squadron of 5th and 10th Native Cavalry, 600 3rd Irregular Cavalry, HM 31st Regiment and the 32nd Native

Heroic conduct of four privates at Mazeena. The Army of Retribution reached Jalalabad in April 1842, staying there until August before moving on to Kabul. During that time there were a number of skirmishes with Afghan tribesmen in the surrounding countryside. A small force successfully engaged with Shinwari tribesmen at Mazeena – over two days of fighting 11 British were killed and 31 wounded. (Anne S. K. Brown Military Collection, Brown University)

British prisoners in captivity. British women and children and some married officers were taken hostage during the retreat from Kabul. Conditions were tough, though they were reasonably well treated. This is the only contemporary picture that includes one of the British children. (© Peter & Renate Nahum)

Infantry, together with 17 guns and sappers. By September they had reached Tezin, along the route of the Kabul retreat.

Akbar Khan had returned to the area from Kabul where he had successfully laid siege to Fatteh Jang, Shah Soojah's successor, and appointed himself *wazir*, and effective head of state. He attempted peace negotiations with Pollock on condition that he would halt the march to Kabul but was rebuffed. A major battle then took place at Tezin on 13 September with Akbar Khan amassing some 16,000 men, and it could have been a disaster for the British since they were now encamped in a valley surrounded by hills occupied by Afghan forces. However, the British had learnt from the military errors of previous years, and avoided defensive squares while adopting more aggressive tactics in pursuing the enemy. British cavalry successfully engaged the Afghan cavalry who had entered the valley, while the infantry scaled the heights and engaged in close-combat bayonet charges. The Afghans dispersed with Akbar Khan retreating northwards beyond Kabul.

As the Army of Retribution was closing in on Kabul, the British prisoners persuaded one of their captors to release them. A day later, on 17 September 1842, they were met by an advance rescue party, led by Captain Shakespear. The map he used at the time is shown on page 34. (Anne S. K. Brown Military Collection, Brown University)

Pollock then proceeded unopposed on to Kabul, reaching the outskirts on 15 September, and two days later Nott arrived with his forces. Nott too had had success, defeating a large force of Afghans near Ghazni, and retaking the city. On 17 September a rescue party met the British prisoners (now consisting of ten women, 11 children, and some 85 soldiers) – a few days before, the prisoners had managed to persuade their captors to release them after almost nine months in captivity. There then followed a two-week period of delicate politics and punitive action. Most of the tribal chiefs who had initiated the insurrection the previous year had left the city, and Pollock negotiated with the Qizilbashis who had remained, and who were largely friendly to the British. He insisted, as had been his orders from Ellenborough, that the British now had no interest in further king-making, and refused requests that a small force should remain to ensure stability. Eventually, it was agreed that Shahpoor, a young Sadozai prince and another son of Shah Soojah, should be installed on the throne. Once again, the tribal divisions within Afghanistan showed themselves, with a message from Afghan leaders to Pollock stating that Shahpoor had been chosen because the Popalzais, Durranis, and Qizilbashis 'cannot exist under the Barokzai'.

Pollock clearly felt that he was authorized to impose some form of retribution on the country. The town of Istalif, some 18 miles north-west of Kabul, had been occupied by a number of Afghan leaders and their families retreating from Kabul. Two divisions were sent to attack and destroy the town. This attack was followed by unpleasant scenes of pillaging and the killing of prisoners. Pollock had initially decided to destroy the Bala Hissar but was persuaded that this would only weaken the already fragile position of the new king. Instead, the Great Bazaar was destroyed by gunpowder on 9 and 10 October. A detachment of British troops had been sent to protect the city inhabitants from further attack, but it proved impossible to stop sepoys, many European soldiers and camp followers from entering the city, and carrying out horrific killings, rapes and plunder. As Kaye noted eight years after the event: 'Such excesses as were committed during the last three days of our occupation of Caubul must ever be deplored as all human weakness and wickedness are to be deplored.'

Astley's Circus in London was renowned for mounting spectacular reconstructions of famous military events. Their show in April 1843 was entitled 'Affghanistan War', and hyped up the invasion, the rescue of the prisoners, and the success of the Army of Retribution, while downplaying the disastrous retreat, and the political failures. The audiences cheered. (TS 931.10 v.3, Houghton Library, Harvard University)

EASTER-MONDAY,
April 17th, 1843, the OPENING of
ASTLEY'S
New Royal Amphitheatre of Arts, Westminster Bridge,
MR. BATTY, SOLE PROPRIETOR.

AFFGHANISTAN WAR!
OR, THE REVOLT OF
CABUL!
AND BRITISH
TRIUMPHS IN INDIA.

A Splendid Military Brass Band has been Engaged for the Stage.

River of Cabul & View of the Beymaroo Hills.
CAFILA DRAWN BY THE BRAHUI MULES!
KOHI NOOR, THE HOUSE OF LIGHT!
THE ZUBAR JUNG, THE MIGHTY IN BATTLE.
SPLENDID HALL OF AUDIENCE,
A GRAND MILITARY BRASS BAND,
THE ARMY OF THE INDUS!

FINAL BRITISH WITHDRAWAL FROM AFGHANISTAN

On 1 October, Governor General Ellenborough signed the Simla Proclamation, announcing that the success of the Army of Retribution and the capture of Ghazni and Kabul 'have again attached the opinion of invincibility to the British arms'. However, in future the Government would leave it to the Afghans themselves to create a government: 'To force a sovereign upon a reluctant people would be as inconsistent with the policy as it is with the principles of the British Government.' The wording strangely echoed the Simla Manifesto that had launched the Afghan invasion and which had been issued by his predecessor Lord Auckland on the very same day four years earlier, and ironically – and perhaps deliberately –signed in the very same room.

On 12 October 1842, the combined armies left Kabul to march back to India through the Khyber Pass, and despite some casualties to the rearguard through harassment from tribesmen, reached Ferozepur in mid-December where a celebratory parade was held before Lord Ellenborough. Akbar Khan had in the meantime returned to Kabul, where he assumed control, and imprisoned Shah Soojah's son Prince Shahpoor, the nominated king, while awaiting the return of his father. Dost Mohammad had been released from house arrest in India, and resumed his throne in 1843. He spent the next 20 years until his death gradually unifying the country to its present borders, and laying the basis for a professional national army. A treaty of friendship was signed with Britain in 1857.

The military success of the Army of Retribution and the withdrawal from Afghanistan was greeted in England with relief. Indeed, the whole venture was celebrated by the 1843 spectacular at Astley's Circus entitled *Affghanistan War – Revolt in Caubul – British Triumphs in India*', with the programme downplaying the actual retreat from Kabul while highlighting the rescue of the British prisoners and Pollock's victories. Nevertheless, military and political

Ferozepur Old Fort. In November 1838 the British forces had assembled on the plains to the west of the Punjab city of Ferozepur ready for the invasion of Afghanistan. A year later British cantonments were set up two miles south of the city, and in December 1842 a great victory parade was held before the Governor General to welcome back the Army of Retribution. (Author's collection)

Sir John Hobhouse (later Lord Broughton) was a Whig politician and President of the Board of Control between 1835 and 1841, a position of key influence in the build-up to the invasion. He later vigorously defended the Government's overall Afghan strategy, but he had criticized Auckland and Macnaughten's decision to reduce the number of troops following the occupation of Kabul. (Author's collection)

scapegoats were sought. Pottinger, as the senior political officer who had signed the final agreement concerning the withdrawal of the forces at Kabul, was brought before a court of inquiry, convened to investigate his conduct, but he was exonerated. On 20 January 1843 Brigadier Shelton was subject to a court marshal, found not guilty on three counts which included using disrespectful language to Elphinstone within hearing of his troops, and making preparations for the retreat without authority. He was found guilty of just one charge of corresponding with Akbar Khan to obtain forage for his horses while negotiations were taking place for the withdrawal, but the court decided he had been censured at the time by Elphinstone and no further action was needed.

In Parliament, the Tories, led by a young Disraeli, had tried to make capital of the military and political failure of the venture that had been mounted by the previous Whig Government, and focussed their scorn on Lord Auckland as the instigator of the invasion. However, they were robustly reminded by Sir John Hobhouse, former President of the Board of Control, that the whole Cabinet had been fully supportive of Lord Auckland's policies, and that the Tories when in opposition had endorsed the invasion at the time. The motion of censure was lost overwhelmingly. Back in India, the British proceeded to consolidate their northern frontiers. The Amirs of Sind unsuccessfully tried to resist continuing British occupation of their territories, and the region passed to British control in 1843. Following the defeat of the Sikhs in the Second Anglo-Sikh War, the Punjab was similarly annexed, and Dost Mohammad signed a treaty acknowledging British possession of the region. The boundaries of British India now touched upon Afghanistan, but by then the British had secured friendly relations with Russia, and the policy of non-interference with Afghanistan remained sacrosanct. The status quo would remain for another 40 years, until Russian ambitions in central Asia were once again seen to threaten British interests, and Britain launched a new invasion of Afghanistan to depose its then ruler, Dost Mohammad's son.

Field Marshall Sir Gerald Templer (1898–1971), in command of the effective campaign in Malaya against counterinsurgents in the 1950s, wrote in 1966 of the First Afghan War that it demonstrated 'the impossibility of controlling, by force of arms alone, a country where the mass of the people are against the "foreigner." It could perhaps be said that lesson has not yet been entirely learnt in the modern world.' His words, written 50 years ago and with the US involvement in the Vietnam War clearly in mind, continue to have contemporary relevance.

THE BATTLEFIELD TODAY

Kabul has grown beyond all recognition, and the city extends well past its boundaries of the 1840s. The Bala Hissar remained the seat of the royal palace following the return of Dost Mohammad but the lower buildings suffered severe damage during the Second Afghan War (1878–81) though the walls were later strengthened by the British shortly before they left. The poor condition of the building persuaded the then Amir Abdur Raham to build a new palace in 1880, and the Bala Hissar was subsequently used as a base for the Afghan army. During the war between rival factions in the 1990s, it was a key focus of conflict and was extensively damaged by bombing. The remains of the upper walls, though, together with abandoned tanks and other weapons, are still visible, though the site is out of bounds to visitors as it is manned by the Afghan National Army.

The house where Burnes was murdered has long been lost to modern development, while the road between the old city and British cantonments is now the main road to the international airport. The cantonments were destroyed by the Afghans after the British force left in 1842, but their location is still a military area and contains the headquarters of modern military forces. The site of the Shah Bagh Gardens, which provided such effective cover for the Afghans allowing them to prevent the British sending rescue missions to the besieged commissariat, now contains the presidential palace and other government offices.

The Bala Hissar in 2007. The lower part of the Bala Hissar, the old fortress occupied by Afghan kings, suffered extensive damage during the Second Afghan War. It was further damaged during recent internal conflicts, but the remains still give a good impression of the dominant position it held over the city. (Bill Woodburn)

Kabul has grown well beyond the boundaries of the city the British invaded. However, this view from the Bala Hissar taken in 2005 still has echoes of Atkinson's illustration from a similar position (see page 51), and the remains of the Russian tank is a salutary reminder of later foreign interventions that were equally unsuccessful. (Bill Woodburn)

The old citadel in Ghazni was largely destroyed by the British and never rebuilt to its former glory. However, much of Ghazni's old walls remain standing, and the sheer scale of the defensive structures that faced the British forces in 1839 are still very much apparent as can be seen in this 1972 photo. (Bill Woodburn)

The Beymaru Heights, where Brigadier Shelton was defeated shortly before the British agreed terms of surrender, is now known as Bibi Mahru Hill, and is a popular spot for walking and kite flying. On top of the hill is an Olympic-size swimming pool, built by the Russians during their occupation, which has been empty for many years.

Herat is the third largest city in Afghanistan with a current population of nearly half a million. The old citadel and walls suffered great neglect, but were restored by UNESCO between 1976 and 1979, and restoration continues under the auspices of the Aga Khan foundation. Having been used in the past by the military as an ammunition dump, the citadel is now open to visitors.

Kandahar, Afghanistan's second largest city, was greatly modernized in the 1930s and 1950s. The defensive 30-foot walls that surrounded the city at the time of the First Afghan War were largely demolished during this period, although some small sections still exist. Between 1994 and 2001 it served as the capital for the Taliban government.

Ghazni is now a modern trading centre and many sections of the old walls remain standing. Its old citadel was largely destroyed by the British during the First Afghan War and was subsequently rebuilt, but never to its former glory. It is now occupied by the Afghan army and is not open to visitors.

Jalalabad continued as a garrison town and was captured by the Taliban in 1996. Now the major city of eastern Afghanistan, its mild winter climate made it a popular retreat for Afghan rulers, and it continues to have a reputation as a green city. The old walls have long been lost to modern development.

The landscape of the route of the retreat of the British forces from Kabul to Jalalabad has hardly changed, but in the current situation remains largely too dangerous for all but the most intrepid traveller. The most detailed recent account of the route was given by the American anthropologist Dr Louis Dupree who walked the retreat in 1963 in order to explore how traditions of oral history in Afghan villages had developed. He left Kabul on 6 January, as had the British forces, and each day covered the exact distance they travelled 123 years earlier. The name of Macnaughten still featured heavily in stories told by village elders, although some said it was he and not Dr Brydon who had been the last European survivor. At Jagdalak Pass, Dr Dupree found wild holly still growing – the holly that the Afghans had used to block the pass with such destructive effect so many years before. The approach he made to the village of Gandamak would have been much as the remnants of the 44th saw it after they had survived the horrors of the Pass, and the small rocky hill on which they made their last stand remained unchanged.

The near final destruction of the British forces took place in Jagdalak Pass. Hundreds were killed in Afghan attacks as they tried to break through a six-foot high holly bush barrier. This 1963 photograph gives an impression of the pass as it would have appeared to the few survivors who managed to get through. (Photo by Louis Dupree, permission of Nancy Hatch Dupree on behalf of the Afghanistan Centre at Kabul University)

Approaching the village of Gandamak, the remnants of the 44th Foot who had survived the Jagdalak Pass must have thought they were now only 35 miles from safety in Jalalabad. However, they were rapidly surrounded, refused to surrender, and made a last stand on a small hill just outside the village. This 1963 photo shows the approach to the village. (Photo by Louis Dupree, permission of Nancy Hatch Dupree on behalf of the Afghanistan Centre at Kabul University)

Gandamak Hill was the small rocky hill outside Gandamak village on which the 44th made their last stand. This picture was taken by Tim Lynch of Freerange International in October 2008, despite the area remaining highly dangerous for foreigners. (Tim Lynch, Freerange International)

BIBLIOGRAPHY AND FURTHER READING

Contemporary and near contemporary

Durand, Henry, *First Afghan War and its Causes*, Longmans, Green & Co, London (1879)

Eyre, Lieutenant Vincent, *Military Operations at Caubul*, John Murray, London (1843)

Forbes, Archibald, *The Afghan Wars, Seeley & Co., London* (1892)

Gleig, Rev. George Robert, *With Sale's Brigade in Afghanistan*, John Murray, London (1846)

Havelock, Henry, *Narrative of the War in Afghanistan* Indus, Karachi (1840)

Hough, William, *March and Operations of the Army of the Indus,* W.Thacker & Co, Calcutta (1841)

Kaye, Sir John, *History of the War in Afghanistan,* Richard Bentley, London (1851)

Kashmiri, Mohan Lal, *Life of Amir Dost Mohammad of Kabul*, Longmans, Green & Co (1846)

Ram, Sita, (translated Norgate, Lt Col), *From Sepoy to Subedar,* Victoria Press, Lahore (1873)

Sale, Lady Florentia, *Journal of the Afghan War*, John Murray, London (1843)

Heyward Stocquelar, Joachim, *Memoirs and Correspondence of Major-General Nott*, Hurst and Blackett, London (1854)

More recent

Dalrymple, William, *Return of a King*, Bloomsbury, London (2013)

Everett, Sir Henry, *History of the Somerset Light Infantry 1685–1914,* Naval and Military Press, Uckfield (1934)

Fremont-Barnes, Gregory, *The Anglo-Afghan Wars 1839–1919*, Osprey Publishing, Oxford (2009)

Heathcote, T. A., *The Afghan Wars 1839–1919*, The History Press, Stroud (2003)

Hopkins, B. D., *The Making of Modern Afghanistan*, Palgrave Macmillan, London (2008)

Johnson, Robert, *The Afghan Way of War*, Oxford University Press, Oxford (2012)

Macrory, Patrick, *Signal Catastrophe*, Hodder & Stoughton, London (1966)

Noelle, Christine, *State and Tribe in Nineteenth-Century Afghanistan – The Reign of Amir Dost Muhammed Khan*, Curzon, Richmond (1997)

Norris, J. A., *The First Afghan War*, Cambridge University Press, Cambridge (1967)

Pottinger, George & Macrory, Patrick, *The Ten-Rupee Jezail – Figures in the First Afghan War*, Michael Russell Publishing, Norwich (1993)

Reshita, Sayed, *Between Two Giants*: *Political History of Afghanistan in the Nineteenth Century,* Afghan Jehad Works, Translation Centre (1990)

Waller, John, *Beyond the Khyber Pass: The Road to Disaster in the First Afghan War,* Random House, New York (1990)

INDEX

Kabul 48, 49, 50; and march 36, 37, 38, 39, 40
Khojak Pass 33, 38
Khord Kabul Pass 73, 76, **77**
Khyber Pass 9, 10, 17, 33, 48; and Ghilzais 56–57; and Pollock 83–85
Kohistan 8, 48, 54

Ludhiana 16
Lugmani 57

Mackenzie, Colin 20
Macnaughten, Sir William 16, 17, 20–21, 22; and insurrection 65, 68; and Kabul 49–50, 51, 52, 54–55, 56, 58, 59; and march 36, 38, 40; and withdrawal 70, 71–72
Madras 12
Mahmud Shah 8, 14, 24, 25
Mahomed Shereef 59, 64, 65
medals **43**
Mehrab, Khan of Kalat 37, 38
Mohammed Zaman Khan Barakzai 71

Napoleon Bonaparte 13
Nepal 15, 83
Nott, Gen William 12, 21, 22–23, 37; and Kabul 58, 59, 67, 88; and Kandahar 41, 52, 82, 85–86
Nuristanis 7

Palmer, Col 57
Palmerston, Lord 50
Pashtuns 7, 33
Paul I of Russia, Czar 13

Payinda Khan 8, 25
Peel, Sir Robert 83
Persia 5, 9, 10, 13–14, 16; and Herat 31, 33, 41, 50
Peshawar 9–10, 15, 17, 24
Pitt the Younger, William 11
Pollock, Gen Sir George 6, 23, 83–88
polygamy 7
Pottinger, Eldred 31, **32**, 57, 72, 73, 90
Punjab, the 7, 9, 50, 90

Qizilbashis 7, 8, 65, 88
Quetta 37

Ranjit Singh 9–10, 14, 15, 24, 50; and Britain 16–17, 32, 33
Roberts, Brig 52
Robertson, Sgt 46
Russia 5, 10, 13, 31, 49–50, 90
Russian-Persian War (1826–28) 14

Sadozais 7–8, 14, 24
Sale, Gen Sir Robert 46, 47, 54, 57, 82; and Kabul 59, 68
Sale, Lady **77**
Second Afghan War (1878–81) 91
Second Anglo-Sikh War (1849) 90
Seeah Sung hills 58–59, 65, 67
Shah Bagh Gardens 59, 64, 65, 69, 91
Shahpoor 88, 89
Shakespear, Capt **87**
Shelton, Brig 22, 56, 58–59, 65, 66–67, 68–69; and investigation 90
Shikarpur 17

Shinwari tribe **86**
Sikhs 9–10, 15, 17, 26, 30, 90
Simla Manifesto 17, 27, 31, 48
Simla Proclamation (1842) 89
Sind 7, 8, 10, 15, 17, 90
Soojah al Mulk, Shah 5, 8, 9, 24, 37; and assassination 82; and Bengal Army 27–28, 30; and Britain 16, 17, 31–32; and Ghazni 41, 43, 46; and Kabul 48–51, **55**, 58–59, 65, 70–71; and Kandahar 39–40
Sturt, Lt 52
supplies 34, 36–38, 40

Tajiks 7
Talbot, Capt **81**
Taliban, the 29, 92
Templer, FM Sir Gerald 90
Tezin 73, 76, 87
Thomson, Capt George **41**, 46
Timur, Prince 28, 30
Treaty of Tilsit (1807) 13
tribes 5, 7–9, 28, 33, 65; and harassment 36, 37–38; and unrest 56–57, 58

Uzbeks 7, 54

Wade, Col Claude 16, 33
Warren, Lt Francis 59, 64, 65
weaponry **28**, **29**, **37**, **81**, **86**
Wellington, Arthur Wellesley, Duke of 12
Willshire, Gen 50

Zaman Khan 82
Zaman Shah 7–8, 24, 25